COAST
AND
SHORE

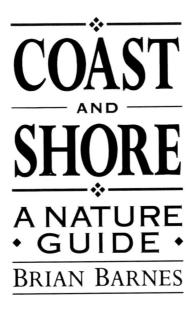

COAST
AND
SHORE
A NATURE
· GUIDE ·
BRIAN BARNES

The Crowood Press

Brian Barnes is Senior Biologist at the Bolton
Institute of Higher Education. A keen
naturalist, he has been widely involved in adult
education, has developed a number of nature
trails and has spent much of his life studying
the seashore.

First published in 1986 by
The Crowood Press
Ramsbury, Marlborough,
Wiltshire SN8 2HE

Reprinted in paperback 1989

British Library Cataloguing in Publication Data

Barnes, Brian
    (British Naturalists' Association guide to coast and
    shore) Coast and Shore
    1. Great Britain. Coastal regions. Organisms
    I. (British Naturalists' Association guide to coast
    and shore) II. Title III. British Naturalists'
    Association
    574.941

    ISBN 1–85223–226–9

Design by Vic Giolitto

Typeset by Quadraset Limited, Midsomer Norton,
Bath, Avon
Printed in Spain by Graficromo s.a., Cordoba

Contents

FOREWORD

Since 1905 the British Naturalists' Association has provided opportunities for beginners and more advanced students of natural history to rub shoulders with experts, both amateur and professional.

Throughout this time its magazine, *Country-Side*, and its local, regional and national meetings have fostered the collection and sharing of knowledge concerning the rocks, soils, plants and animals which make up our living landscape. Essential in this process of national learning and the spreading of awareness about wildlife has been the publication of many identification keys – keys to groups like lichens, plant galls, harvestmen and spiders, which though present and often abundant in most habitats were at one time frequently overlooked or wrongly ignored, because there was no way in, no key to unlock the doors of enquiry. In the same way, the Association's pamphlets entitled 'Let's begin the study of . . .' helped pioneer many branches of field science.

At last, some of that knowledge, the fruit of all those eighty years of unique experience, is now made public in this superb series of books. Habitat by habitat, all is revealed.

Most of my own knowledge of plants and animals was gained in the field by walking with and listening to the 'ologists', the experts in each subject – bryology, ornithology, algology etc, etc. Each trip was an occasion to be remembered thanks to the personal anecdotes and sheer enthusiasm of people who had all the facts at their fingertips and who loved the subject of their expertise.

If you can't go on such trips, these books are the next best thing. Open up the pages and you can almost smell the sweet or rotten smell of a river, see the rooks flying from the beech hangers, and hear the warm buzz of summer insects or the crisp crackle of a winter morning.

If I may be allowed one personal reminiscence. I can remember following John Clegg (the author of the volume on ponds and streams in this series) down to the ponds in the grounds of Haslemere Educational Museum, where he was then curator. *Stratiotes aloides* (water soldier), *Nepa cinerea* (the water scorpion), *Hydrocharis morsus ranae* (frogbit), *Gunnera manicata* (the giant prickly rhubarb from South America). . . . This was the first time I was ever shown these things and I will never forget either the experience or the names.

I am grateful to John Clegg and all the others who led me along the many paths of natural history and to a very full and worthwhile life. I am grateful too to all the officers and members of the British Naturalists' Association, both past and present, for everything they have done and are doing to share their knowledge and wonder of life.

What a super series of books! The only problem is what is the B.N.A. going to do to celebrate its centenary?

David Bellamy

President of the Youth Section of
the British Naturalists' Association
Bedburn, County Durham

 **British Naturalists' Association**

The British Naturalists' Association has existed since 1905, when E. Kay Robinson founded the B.N.A.'s journal *Country-Side* and groups of readers began to hold meetings which gave amateur naturalists an opportunity to meet experts and to discuss topics of mutual interest with them. It is this network of branches all over Britain that forms the basis of the B.N.A. New members are always welcome and enquiries regarding membership should be addressed to Mrs June Pearton, 48 Russell Way, Higham Ferrers, Northamptonshire NN9 8EJ.

During its eighty years of existence many distinguished naturalists and public figures have been associated with the B.N.A. At present the President is Lord Skelmersdale, the President of the Youth Section is David Bellamy, and Professor J.L. Cloudsley-Thompson, R.S.R. Fitter, David Hosking, Eric Hosking, Alfred Leutscher, Professor Kenneth Mellanby, Angela Rippon, Sir Peter Scott, Professor Sir Richard Southwood, Sir George Taylor and H.J. Wain are Vice-Presidents of the Association.

Country-Side appears four times a year and publishes articles about every aspect of natural history. Contributions, including photographs and drawings, should be addressed to Ron Freethy, The Editor, *Country-Side*, Thorneyholme Hall, Roughlee, Nr Burnley, Lancashire BB12 9LH.

1 LAND, SEA AND SHORE

The sea

Whether it is the gentle breaking of waves upon a summer shore or pillars of spray from storm waves in a winter gale, the sight and sound of the sea can be soothing or stirring, inviting or frightening. Whoever you are and whatever your mood, almost certainly you will react to it.

What is this element which repels and draws us? A watery fluid that tastes of salt? A fluctuating liquid perimeter to the land which trundles the plastic and organic debris of last week's sewage discharge up the beach? A medium for transport from one land mass to another? An apparently ever-bountiful resource which provides us with food? It is all these and much more. But the sea in which we paddle or swim is usually an adulterated version of the real thing, diluted by fresh water trickling down cliffs, thrusting forth in turbulent streams from some ravine or discharging from a great estuary which produces brackish conditions for miles up and down the coast. To find the real thing a boat trip two or three miles offshore may be necessary.

This real sea differs from that in which we bathe on our summer holiday. It is undiluted, a denser medium made up of a solution of salts. Common salt – sodium and chlorine (in the form of chloride) – is responsible for its salty taste; its slightly bitter taste is due to other salts, such as magnesium; and a whole host of other elements are present – calcium, potassium, iron, sulphates, nitrates, phosphates, carbonates and bicarbonates. Oxygen is dissolved in it and a whole range of trace elements are present in minute quantities, including silver and gold.

At marine biology stations, such as Plymouth in the south and Port Erin in the Isle of Man, regular offshore samples of sea water are taken and analysed. Typical results of such an analysis are:

Cations		Anions	
Na^+	77%	Cl^-	90%
Mg^{2+}	18%	SO_4^{2-}	9%
Ca^{2+}	3%	$HCO_3{}_-$	1%
K^+	2%		

This rich mineral solution should be an ideal medium for plant growth. Away from the shading clouds of industrial pollution the bright sun can strike through; the constant motion of the water ensures high levels of dissolved oxygen; and, even with the addition of some acid rain, the buffering action of such a rich solution maintains a constant pH value around neutral. Moreover, the currents from the Gulf Stream bring a supply of relatively warm water.

But where are the plants? If you take a conical net of fine bolting silk (a plain-weave fabric with a high number of threads per centimetre) with a sample tube attached to the tapered end and tow it slowly, suitably weighted, just below the surface of the water for 200 or 300 metres (650–1,000 feet) you will discover them. An examination of the sample tube will be at once exciting and revealing. The sparkling water is full of tiny plants, some barely visible to the naked eye, in a variety of shades and colours.

These small, single-celled plants are known as phytoplankton, from the Greek words

The sea – source of nutrients for so many food webs of our oceans, beaches and coasts.

phuton (plant) and *plagos* (wandering). They are buoyed up by the dense sea water, but further buoyancy aids within the cells in the form of air bubbles and oil droplets serve to reduce the density of their bodies. The fine branch-like structures rising out of the cell walls of some species also offer resistance to the water and prevent sinking; while the fine microscopic whiplike threads of other forms beat the water and serve the same function. It is important that the plants stay in the surface layers of the water, as the surface light soon fades with increasing depth and these plants, like those on the land, must have sufficient light in order to manufacture food. The beautiful colours of phytoplankton are due to their yellow-brown, yellow-green or bright green pigments, which vary according to their group. The pigments trap light energy and use it to drive the food manufacturing

process known as photosynthesis.

With such an ample supply of mineral salts, dissolved carbon dioxide and water, given a reasonable temperature these plants (which include diatoms, desmids and tiny green flagellates) can grow and reproduce at a great rate. The number of phytoplankton in the water is vast, an estimate of 727,000 per cubic metre (20,000 per cubic foot) being regarded as quite acceptable. With such a large harvest being constantly produced it would indeed be strange if animals able to exploit this abundant food resource had not evolved.

A somewhat coarser-meshed net trawled through the sea at walking speed for five minutes or so will provide a haul of tiny animals no less fascinating than the phytoplankton. These are the zooplankton, animals which wander haphazardly in the body of the sea, drifting in tidal currents rather than moving under their own steam. Their limbs and movements serve only to maintain or change their depth in the water. Not being dependent on light for their food,

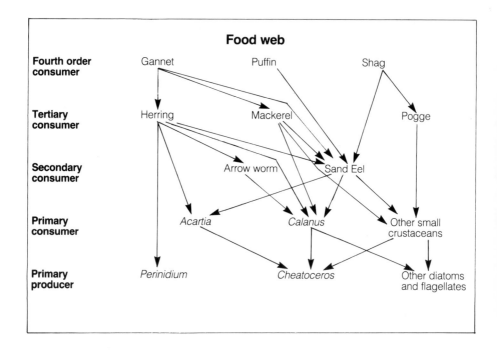

Food web

Fourth order consumer	Gannet	Puffin	Shag
Tertiary consumer	Herring	Mackerel	Pogge
Secondary consumer		Arrow worm	Sand Eel
Primary consumer	*Acartia*	*Calanus*	Other small crustaceans
Primary producer	*Perinidium*	*Cheatoceros*	Other diatoms and flagellates

Below Common scurvy grass (*Cochleria officinalis*).

they are not confined to the upper ten fathoms of the sea (like the plants), but are found at various levels, many only coming nearer to the surface at night to feed on the phytoplankton.

Zooplankton originate from a wide variety of major animal groups. Many are microscopic, single-celled animals with chalky shells, including the Foramenifera and Radiolaria, but there are also tiny jellyfish and sea gooseberries, shrimp-like crustaceans, the eggs or larvae of marine worms and crabs, those of molluscs such as cockles or periwinkles, and the eggs and fry of many fish, such as herring, mackerel, haddock and plaice.

Marine food webs

Zooplankton graze on the phytoplankton and in turn may become food items for larger members of the zooplankton. These predatory zooplankton are preyed on in turn by herring and larger fish, such as basking sharks and whales, and the smaller fish may be eaten by sea birds – sand eels, for example, form a major part in the diet of the shag. The whole of this food web is based on phytoplankton. As one moves from one feeding level to the next, the number of organisms is reduced, but body size increases. However, it is not the difference in number or body size that is important, but the amount of energy transferred from one feeding level to another. For it is the efficiency of this process that determines the population of top predators supported by the food webs. All the plants and the animals in the food web must burn up some of the material they have captured in the process of respiration to drive vital body processes such as movement. This represents energy that is unavailable to the next feeding level, and in the case of the animals voided undigested material represents an energy loss to the system too. Furthermore organisms that escape predation will ultimately die – a third way in which energy is lost from this particular system. In fact only about 10 per cent of

Flowering shoots of sea campion (*Silene maritima*).

the total energy entering one feeding level is available to the next.

However, although the undigested material and dead plants and animals escape this system, as they sink to the ocean bed they are decomposed by bacteria and much of the raw material and mineral salts making up their bodies is released and becomes available for recycling. Alternatively the dead organisms may be eaten by carrion feeders, or may be partially decomposed and incorporated into the ocean bed sediments. Eventually, these may be converted into oil many millions of years after they have been entombed.

Many of the organisms which are permanent members of the zooplankton feed, reproduce and complete their life-cycles while drifting in the sea. They may sometimes sink to the ocean bed where they form food for bottom-living or benthic animals, such as starfish, marine worms and sea anemones, which in turn form the food of fish including cod.

Many larval animal forms, however, are only temporary members of the zooplankton, taking advantage of the vast food supply for rapid growth. Being carried by sea currents enables them to be widely distributed, thus providing opportunities to colonise new territories. If they are eaten or are carried to unfavourable areas, they will not survive as individuals. However, the high level of fertile egg production has great advantages for the species as a whole. Fish larvae feed on different food items according to their size, an adaptation which reduces competition for a food resource within a species.

In his book *The Open Sea* Sir Alistair Hardy reviews the feeding habits of different size/age groups of herring. He describes how once a herring reaches a length of about 2·5–4·5cm (1–1¾ inches) it develops silvery scales and

eventually can swim strongly enough to become independent of ocean currents. Such fish are known as nekton, from the Greek *nektos* (swimming). Subsequently the younger fish of the species such as herring and sprat form huge shoals, which are, for example, found in the Wash and the Thames estuary, where they are caught and sold as whitebait.

Fish larvae developing in the zooplankton are of two types. Those which spend the rest of their lives in the upper layers of the sea, such as herring and mackerel, are known as pelagic animals. In contrast, the larvae of plaice, dab, cod and whiting ultimately end up as bottom-living or demersal forms.

The entire marine ecosystem is driven by the energy of the sun. The sun's energy is captured by the phytoplankton, which either directly or indirectly form a food resource that supports animal life in the open sea or on the ocean floor. It also supports species which to a greater or lesser extent spend time on land. Sea birds are particularly important in this

Puffin with sand eels.

respect, as are seals, while the ultimate exploiter of the system is, of course, man.

The land

Most people find islands both mysterious and intriguing – and for the naturalist there is a great pleasure in searching every nook and cranny, discovering new plants and animals and renewing acquaintance with those previously found. Among my own favourite islands are Craigleith and Bass Rock in the Firth of Forth, off North Berwick. An annual pilgrimage there in the second week of May has been my joy for many years now, but the study of any island is a rewarding experience. Arriving at North Berwick, our first sight is of a great volcanic plug towering into the sky – known locally as the 'law' – with its crown of whale jawbones, a possible testimony to the one-time trade of local seafarers. After supper in the fading light we look out over the sea, dominated by the Bass, hoping for good weather and landing conditions on the following morning. The strident calls of oystercatchers and redshanks echo along the beach and a small flotilla of eider ducks gives promise of the delights in store.

The next morning, duly breakfasted and provisioned, we eagerly negotiate the slopes down to our mooring. We soon gather our sea legs as we turn the headland and move across the calm waters into the sun, with Bass Rock drawing ever nearer. As we go, a low-flying green cormorant or shag flaps its way over the water. The shag can be distinguished from its relative the cormorant by its lack of white cheek patches and its prominent head tuft. Farther from land, a small flock of guillemots duck below the surface as we close with them. Soon we observe our first gannet wheeling in the sky and plunging vertically, with wings spread, into the sea.

Later the great bulk of Bass Rock towers above us, its rockface whitened by the droppings of some 13,000 pairs of gannets. We steer a one mile circuit round this great rock,

observing the guillemots and razorbills on the narrow ledges, and in a deep cleft to the west of the island sight a huge community of kittiwakes clinging precariously in pairs to even smaller ledges. Indeed, these ledges are so narrow that to raise a family of even a single youngster seems an impossible feat. On the cliff tops are two or three pairs of fulmars, recognised by the salt gland on their beaks and their black eyelashes. In the air the fulmar can be distinguished by the straightness of its wing and its gliding flight.

Rounding the east of the island, adjacent to a long flight of concrete steps, the black igneous rock shows through, emphasising the coloured beaks and black and white plumage of groups of puffins, which take flight as we disembark. With the boat rising and falling among floats of dabberlocks and oarweed exposed by the low tide, the surfacing of a curious seal provokes gasps of excitement. The climb up the unguarded steps takes us past anchored seaweeds, bands of mussels and barnacles and finally black lichen, arranged in successive horizontal belts.

Island plants

Bass Rock, despite its exciting bird life, is not such a rich repository of plants but, as one would expect on a small island, those present have an intimate relationship with the surrounding sea. In 1980 a list of seventeen species was made, though this was not exhaustive. Two characteristic plants which favour the mineral-rich environment provided by sea spray and guano are common scurvy grass and sea campion.

Common scurvy grass
Cochlearia officinalis

The thick, fleshy leaves of scurvy grass, which have a waxy surface, are rich in vitamin C and so were eaten by sailors to prevent scurvy. A member of the wallflower family, it aggressively colonises areas of friable rock, cracks in steps and mounds of abandoned

Above Tree mallow (*Lavetera arborea*), close-up of flowering shoots.

Right Red campion (*Melandrium rubrum var zetlandicum*).

gravel. Common scurvy grass produces a blaze of white four-petalled flowers, while Danish scurvy grass (*Cochlearia danica*), a smaller and usually prostrate plant, generally has lilac-coloured flowers.

Sea campion *Silene maritima*

Bedecked in spring by groups of large white flowers with bladdery carmine-veined sepals, the beautiful blue-green cushions of sea campion form a striking contrast with the ledges of dark rock to which they cling. The paired, fleshy leaves are blue-green in colour, due to a waxy covering which protects the plant from excessive water loss in the dehydrating coastal winds.

Tree mallow *Lavatera arborea*

More characteristic of the Mediterranean regions, the tree mallow is typically found in the southern and western coastal regions of this country. It is thought to have been introduced artificially to the east coast. However, it thrives on offshore islands such as Bass and forms dense stands of tree-like plants up to 3m (10 feet) in height. In spring the plants look like a green sea surrounding the islands of white gannet colonies.

Tree mallow occupies the flatter slopes of the island. Its felt-like leaves and young stems are covered with hairs, which help to reduce water loss. These leaves may be up to 20cm (8 inches) or so in diameter and form a dense canopy, below which the green cormorant or shag, and the eider duck sometimes set their nests, away from the predatory eyes of hovering gulls. Indeed, the dead stems of this biennial plant are often used as nesting material by the shag. The pink flowers, about 4cm (1½ inches) in diameter, are edged with purple veins which join to form a dense patch of purple in the flower centre.

Red campion *Melandrium rubrum*

Although I was surprised to find quite large patches of red campion growing on Bass, it is in fact well recorded as a plant characteristic of nitrate-rich bird cliffs. However, the plants found on Bass require particular mention. They have stout, densely hairy stems and the stem leaves are very downy on both sides. The pink flowers are in tight clusters and are quite unlike the usual mainland form of the plant. In their *Flora of the British Isles* Clapham, Tutin and Warburg cite a special form of red campion, *Melandrium rubrum zetlandicum*, also found in the Orkneys and Shetland, and I feel sure these Bass plants are of that type. Red campion more like the typical inland form has also been found on Bass, although the Shetland type still persists and a white-flowered mutant form has been found too. As with tree mallow, the hairiness appears to be an adaptation to ensure water conservation.

Another plant found here similarly adapted is dovesfoot cranesbill (*Geranium molle*), while the alternative adaptation of forming fleshy organs is seen in plants of sorrel (*Rumex acetosa*) and the common sea beet (*Beta maritima*), from which our cultivated beetroot originated. With so much guano around it is not surprising that the ubiquitous nettle is also present.

Many other plants are found on sea cliffs which seem well adapted to maritime conditions. They include sea pink (*Armeria maritima*), sea plantain (*Plantago maritima*), buckshorn plantain (*Plantago coronopus*), rock samphire (*Crithmum maritimum*), alexanders (*Smyrnium olusatrum*), wall pepper or biting stonecrop (*Sedum acre*) and English stonecrop (*Sedum anglica*). Various grasses and lichens are also present.

Birds

If the influence of the sea on the land is reflected in the plant life, this interaction is

Gannets 'scissoring', a pattern of behaviour carried out when one of a pair returns to the nest.

English stonecrop, in full bloom in June.

even more clearly observable in some of the birds.

Gannet *Sula bassana*

The Atlantic gannet or solan goose is the largest British breeding sea bird and is a member of the pelican family. Its fat-laden body provides insulation, enabling it to inhabit the cold, rich waters overlying the continental shelf of north-west Europe. At 3kg (6½lb) it is rather a heavy bird and its weight enables it to plunge-dive for herring and mackerel. These nutritious fish are muscular and powerful, but the large beak and strength of the gannet enables it to handle them, so that it is virtually the only bird to occupy this rich feeding niche. Cormorants (*Phalocrocorax carbo*), although as heavy as gannets, do not forage far enough to compete.

Gannetries are located mainly on the islands in the west and north of Great Britain, from Grassholm in the south-west to Ailsa Craig in the west and St Kilda in the north. Bass Rock was the only east coast gannetry until

Bempton was colonised in the 1930s. (It now has over a hundred breeding pairs.) However, in the Firth of Forth Bass is ideally located, being near to the fishing grounds off the Farne Islands; and even without plunge-diving the gannets can take sprats and sand eels in quantity in St Andrew's Bay and the Tay estuary to the north.

It is this ready supply of food present in quantity at the correct time of year that enables the gannet to pursue its breeding strategy. Its success at Bass may be seen by the increase in nesting sites from 4,820 in 1949 to 13,500 in 1977. However, it must also be said that in the more enlightened times of the second half of this century the reduction in human predation has allowed a general rise in the gannet population. Its island cliff habitat also offers protection from the larger predatory mammals, and the strong updraughts on the cliffs aid it in take-off and landing. Its long pointed beak and tapering tail enable it to enter air and water easily, while its mainly white colour gives it camouflage when fishing.

As well as food, the sea provides oarweed and toothed wrack for nesting material. Grass

Fulmars (*Fulmarus glacilis*) at nest.

from the land, such as red fescue, is also used in nest construction.

The gannet squab hatches from the single egg after forty-three days' incubation, a black reptile-like thing, but it is soon covered in white down. It grows rapidly, tended carefully by at least one parent, so that thirteen weeks after hatching it has become a black-feathered juvenile, heavily laden with fat. This is a critical stage in the life of the gannet, for it now has to negotiate a position from which it can jump-glide into the sea. This in itself can be hazardous and many are killed in the process. The successful ones may glide two to three miles, but once they hit the sea they are unable to rise from the water, so they have to live off their body fat, hopefully learning to feed themselves before they starve. This urge to leave the land is instinctive, and the successful ones may migrate as far as the equatorial waters of north-west Africa. The pressures on survival are great however, and 60–70 per cent of the year's hatch die. Thus the sea, having provided the food resource,

now acts as an agent of natural selection ensuring that only the fittest birds survive.

For two summers the young, together with other immature and adult plumaged non-breeders, wander the sea lanes in extended foraging trips. In its fourth and fifth years the male establishes a site in or at the edge of its former colony, although it may stray from its island of origin. At this stage it 'advertises' for a mate. The females, often a little younger, respond and a pair is formed. The next season they breed for the first time and continue for the rest of their lives (sixteen years or more). During this time the gannet will usually remain faithful to site and mate.

The gannet provides a beautiful illustration of a bird's adaptation to a particular ecological niche, pursuing a lifestyle in which it interacts with both the sea and the land, without involving the frontier to both – the shore. (The term 'ecological niche' encompasses a bird's lifestyle, where it lives, what it feeds on and how it behaves.)

Fulmar *Fulmarus glacialis*

From only one British breeding station at St

Kilda in 1878, the fulmar had extended to 365 nesting sites by 1949. Ornithologists believe that its ability to feed on offal produced by the flensing of whales supplemented its natural diet of planktonic jellyfish, sea gooseberries and crustaceans and aided its spread south. This bird spends three to four years on the open sea after fledging, breeding only at seven years of age.

Green cormorant (shag)
Phalacrocorax aristotelis

Common cormorant
Phalacrocorax carbo

The shag at 65–80cm (26–31 inches) in length is smaller than the cormorant at 90cm (35 inches). It can also be distinguished by its crest (in summer) and the absence of the white cheek patches of the cormorant. These two closely related birds, like the gannet, belong to the pelanicaniformes or pelican family. Despite their similar appearance the birds do not compete with one another, but occupy different ecological niches. Both have the same upright stance and are goose-like in flight, but shags are birds of rocky coasts and deeper water, avoiding the shelving sandy coasts, bays and muddy estuaries favoured by the cormorant, where they are often seen with their wings outstretched to dry. Cormorants are also seen on rivers and lakes, where they are sometimes regarded as a threat to trout fisheries. Indeed, they are not popular with the fishing fraternity since over 95 per cent of the cormorant's diet is made up of food fishes. However, although 40 per cent of its diet is made up of flatfish, only 10 per cent are of marketable size. In contrast the shag takes sand eels and bottom fish such as pogges, spotted dragonets, sea stickleback and pipefish.

The shag is also less gregarious than the cormorant, nesting on sheltered ledges just above the sea's reach, whereas cormorants nest on broad, flat ledges associated with high cliffs and buttresses, although in Ireland some nest in trees.

Common guillemot *Uria aalge*

Razorbill *Alca torda*

Puffin *Fratercula arctica*

These three small auks all dive well, swim with their feet and wings, and are characterised by a low, whirring flight over the water. They also all stand upright on rocky ledges and look penguin-like when on land, to which they return to breed in April or May and stay until August, overwintering at sea. They are mainly fish feeders, though the puffin will take molluscs and crustaceans as well.

Although closely related, they occupy slightly different breeding sites. Common guillemots occupy narrow ledges with no nests, whereas razorbills prefer crevices and puffins, although they will use crevices, prefer

Guillemots (*Uria aalge*).

Adult shag (*Phalacrocorax aristotelis*) – note head tuft and lack of white cheek patches.

burrows. These slightly different breeding niches prevent competition for space between birds with somewhat similar lifestyles.

The difference between their nesting sites is also reflected in the shape of their eggs. The single, blotched guillemot egg, although exposed, is camouflaged and extremely pear-shaped, causing it to roll in a circle if it is blown by the wind — an apparent adaptation to a narrow ledge breeding location. The brown to white egg of the razorbill is less pear-shaped, less obvious, and unlikely to roll much within a crevice. The white egg of the puffin is laid deep in a burrow and is more rounded in shape, the surroundings affording protection from both predators and the elements.

The bill shapes of these three birds would also seem to offer scope for reflection on feeding methods and diet. The slender, pointed beak of the guillemot is distinct from the more blunt and flattened one of the razorbill, a development even more pronounced in the puffin. It would be of great interest to investigate the feeding methods of these birds to see if the bill shapes determine the diet.

At Bass Rock, then, the interaction of both sea and land through the medium of plants and animals can be observed. These living organisms have undergone structural, physiological and behavioural adaptations in order to exploit both environments successfully. So as not to compete with one another, certain species, although similar in appearance, pursue particular lifestyles and strategies to exploit different ecological niches. Some species show a cyclicity of breeding pattern which may occur annually (groundsel), every two years (tree hollyhock) or require a period of maturation which is followed by an annual reproductive cycle utilising resources from both land and sea (sea campion and the birds).

Rocks and climate

This cyclicity of pattern may also be detected in the formation of the materials which make up our cliffs and shores and in the climate which interacts with them. The basaltic rocks that make up much of the shore around North Berwick are volcanic in origin — Bass Rock, for example, is the cone of an extinct volcano active in Cambrian times 400–500 million years ago.

In other coastal situations we have what are known as sedimentary rocks. These are rocks formed from sediments which were slowly deposited, often under shallow sea conditions. This material has hardened under the weight of further deposits to form a characteristic layered or stratified rock. Chalks, shales, mudstones and harder limestones and sandstones are examples of such rocks. Long ago movements of the earth's crust led to these deposits being lifted out of the sea to form cliffs, hills and mountains. In coastal situations both wave action and the carbonic acid created by carbon dioxide dissolving in water erode and dissolve such softer rock, progressively exposing new material. Great excitement and fun can be had searching for fossilised plants and animals in these places and many fossils, because of their similarity to present day marine organisms, support the view that these rocks were formed under the sea.

Southern Dorset is one of the classic sites for finding fossils, for the dark shales of the Charmouth area yielded an ichthyosaurus (fish dinosaur) skeleton in 1811 and later the first pterodactyl skeleton to be discovered in Britain. The beach at Lyme Regis is peppered with ammonites (fossil relatives of squid and cuttlefish) and on some larger limestone boulders set in the beach these can be over 30cm in diameter.

North of Lancaster the carboniferous limestone of Arnside forms low cliffs and beautiful examples of sea lilies or crinoids, which are related to sea urchins and starfish, fairly litter the upper shore. On the east coast the beaches of Scarborough and Robin Hood's Bay are

Fossilised crinoids, Arnside, Lancashire.

rich in fossils and the exposure of petrified, rippled sand and mussel-like bivalves is not uncommon.

Cyclical changes in climate can be of minor or of long-term duration, occurring through decades, centuries, thousands or even millions of years. In prehistoric times over a period of 70–80 million years the climate of north-west Europe gradually cooled through a series of cold and warm cycles from sub-tropical through temperate to the full glacial conditions of the Ice Age. The extension of the ice caps in Britain meant that the Welsh mountains and the uplands of Scotland, northern England and the Lake District were covered with thick ice and the associated glaciers ground and plucked at the underlying rock creating a mixture of pebbles, sand and clay which was left by retreating glaciers as moraine. The ice also moved and often rounded and grooved small and large boulders.

All this morainic material was moved considerable distances from its sites of origin, either directly by the ice or by powerful out-wash streams created when the ice retreated. The boulders and large stones are known as erratics, while the piles of glacial moraine along with the outwash material of glacial streams either partially or completely capped the underlying rock surface. The trapping of so much water as ice on land during cold glacial periods meant that only limited amounts of liquid water returned to the sea at these times. This caused sea levels to fall by around 100m during the last glaciation.

Thus another cycle – the hydrological cycle – by which water is passed from sea to land and returned via streams and rivers is brought into focus. The implications of this ice accumulation for the British Isles were that much of the area now known as the North Sea and the Irish Sea was dry land. The subsequent warm periods caused ice wastage and water was returned to the sea. The resulting rising sea levels led to the erosion of the piles of morainic material, so that much beach material which exists round our coasts today had its origins in this glacial debris.

Precipitation, now falling as rain, and associated weathering action have eroded upland glacial deposits. This has been transported down streams and rivers, being deposited in estuaries and coastal locations, thus adding to the material already present. A further result of melting ice and the changing sea levels is the formation of wave-cut notches in cliff-faces, raised beaches and drowned forests. As the ice melts, the sea level rises and the waves act against rock, cutting notches and creating beaches. The land surface, relieved of the weight of the ice, particularly in mountainous areas like northern Scotland, rises relative to the sea so that raised beaches are formed. Low lying areas of land remote from the sea were colonised by trees at an early stage in the process of ice retreat. Such woodlands may have been gradually overwhelmed by rising sea levels creating the drowned forests sometimes seen at low spring tide levels on various parts of our coasts.

Above Razorbill (*Alca torda*) and young – Lunga, Outer Hebrides.

Above Giant's Causeway, County Antrim.

Below Erosion of upfolded limestone material, Stairhole, Dorset.

Tides

Anyone who has ever been on a seashore is familiar with the phenomenon of tides – that they 'come in' and 'go out'. But few, perhaps, stop to consider what tides are and how they are caused.

Tides are best considered from three time scales: daily, monthly and yearly.

Daily aspects of tides

The earth can be thought of as surrounded by a water jacket held in place by the earth's gravitational pull, as shown in the diagrams. Gravitational pull is also exerted by the moon and this modifies the effect of that of the earth, thus the shape of the water jacket around the earth is modified into an ellipse. The earth rotates on its axis every twenty-four hours and in that time any single point on its surface passes through two high and low tides. As the moon is not stationary, the tides do not occur at the same time every day. In fact, the moon completes a full circuit of the earth, returning to its original position in twenty-eight days or one lunar month.

Monthly aspects of tides

As well as the moon, the sun also exerts a weak but significant influence on the tides. During the lunar month there are two distinctive periods. The gravitational pulls of the sun and moon may either be in line, thus reinforcing each other, or they may be at right angles to one another, tending to cancel each other out. The combined gravitational pull of the sun and moon gives rise to particularly high tides, known as spring tides. (Here the word 'spring' has nothing to do with the seasons, but is derived from the Old English word *sprungum*, meaning flood tide.) When the sun and moon pull at right angles to each other the resulting high tides are lower. These are known as neap tides, derived from the Old English word *nepflod*, meaning 'scarcely advancing'.

Thus in a lunar month there will be two

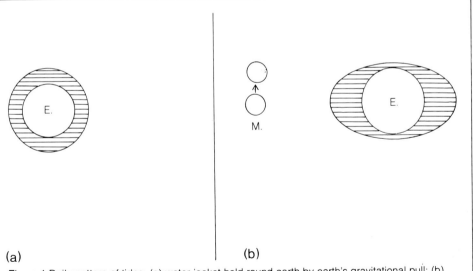

(a)   (b)

Figure 1 Daily pattern of tides: (a) water jacket held round earth by earth's gravitational pull; (b) water jacket distorted into ellipse by gravitational pull of moon. Thus, as the earth rotates on its axis every 24 hours, a single point on its surface passes through two high and two low tides; during this time the moon will have moved $1/28$ of its circuit round the earth.

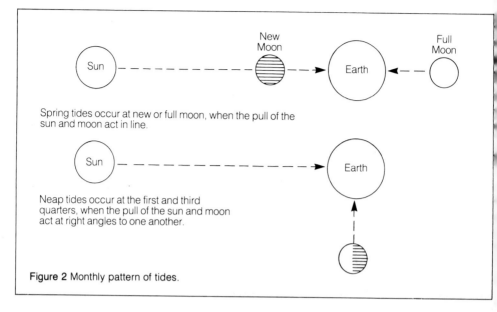

Spring tides occur at new or full moon, when the pull of the sun and moon act in line.

Neap tides occur at the first and third quarters, when the pull of the sun and moon act at right angles to one another.

Figure 2 Monthly pattern of tides.

periods (the first and third quarters of the moon) of lowish neap tides alternating with two periods (new and full moon) of spring tides.

Annual aspects of tides

The earth revolves round the sun, but its path follows an ellipse, not a circle. It follows that there will be two periods when the earth is nearer the sun. These are the equinoxes. During the equinoxes, since the sun is nearer to the earth, its gravitational pull is greater; therefore the spring tides occurring during the equinoxes are the highest of the year. Thus spring tides do occur in the season of spring, but they occur in autumn as well. Spring tides also occur in the mid-summer and mid-winter months, but as the sun is then further from the earth and its gravitational pull is correspondingly weaker, these spring tides are never as high as those which occur during the spring and autumn equinoxes.

On gravitational and meteorological grounds, one can expect two high tides and two low tides each day. This is known as the semi-diurnal tidal rhythm. However, because of headlands and the funnelling effect of coastal inlets, changing depths of water in different parts of the world, frictional forces and the natural periods of oscillation of the oceans' basins, the tidal period can vary. In the Gulf of Mexico, for example, local conditions produce only one tide per day. In other places – for example at Great Yarmouth, in parts of Dorset and Hampshire and in the Sound of Jura in the Western Isles – three or four tides can occur in a day. Under certain conditions tides can also be influenced by barometric pressure and strong onshore winds, which may delay the time and extent of the tidal ebb. It is, therefore, imperative that naturalists and party leaders, wildfowlers and sea anglers familiarise themselves with local tide patterns, particularly if a visit is planned to an unfamiliar area. Reference to local tide tables is essential.

Tidal range

If the graph of tidal oscillations is examined, the tidal heights through both spring and

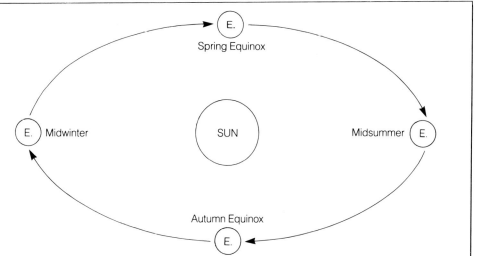

Figure 3 Annual aspects of tides. At the equinoxes the sun is nearer the earth than in midsummer and midwinter; its gravitational pull is therefore greater and the equinoctial spring tides are the highest.

neap phases can be seen. The height in metres/ feet shown at the side of the graph could be thought of as corresponding to the scale of a harbour master's gauge. Note that, between 20 July and 23 July we have a phase of spring tides. These high tides of around

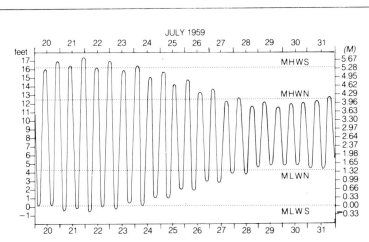

Figure 4 Graph showing tidal oscillations. The period 20–22 July is one of spring tides, that of 28–30 July is one of neap tides (after Lewis 1972). Key to abbreviations: EHWST – Extreme High Water Spring Tide; MHWST – Mean High Water Spring Tide; MHWNT – Mean High Water Neap Tide; MTL – Mean Tide Level; MLWNT – Mean Low Water Neap Tide; MLWST – Mean Low Water Spring Tide; ELWST – Extreme Low Water Spring Tide.

Holy Island, beach of rock and shingle.

4·57–5·18m (15–17 feet) also show the greatest fall, to between 0·0–0·3m (0–1 foot). Thus with spring tides we experience the greatest tidal range. In a similar way the neap tides occurring between 28 July and 31 July show the smallest range, rising to around 3·35–3·65m (11–12 feet) and falling to around 1·22m or 1·52m (4–5 feet).

Only during spring tides is the highest part of the beach immersed and the lowest part of the beach exposed. This has important implications for the distribution of animals and plants over the shore. Seaweeds such as channelled wrack can survive with only limited immersion by the sea and are found on the upper region of the shore, while the great oarweeds are exposed only during low spring tides. Similarly, the small periwinkle (*Littorina neritoides*) is found in the spray zone of the high spring tides, while the dahlia anemone (*Tealia felina*) is found associated with the holdfasts of the oarweeds. Because of this, certain shore organisms appear to be arranged in zones or belts at right angles to the tidal movement. As the period of exposure and submergence are important to the survival and lifestyle of shore organisms, it is useful to ascertain the annual average or mean levels of high and low, spring and neap tides. These are shown by dotted lines on the graph showing tidal oscillations:

Mean High Water Spring (MHWS) = 4·57m (15 feet)
Mean High Water Neap (MHWN) = 3·81m (12½ feet)
Mean Low Water Neap (MLWN) = 1·22m (4 feet)
Mean Low Water Spring (MLWS) = 0·0m (0 feet).

These provide useful reference points from which to describe the distribution of the beach flora and fauna.

At the equinoxes the highest and the lowest spring tides of the year occur and the greatest tidal range is experienced. Such tides are known as the Extreme High Water (EHWS) and Extreme Low Water (ELWS) for spring tides. On these occasions sand hoppers (which do not like immersion) can be seen migrating up the beach away from the advancing tide. It is also possible at low tide to find depressions in the sand which lead into the burrows of razor shells (*Ensis* spp).

Tidal range also varies from one part of the coast to another. The Bristol Channel, for example, has a maximum tidal range of up to 16m (52 feet), while at Portland and around the Isle of Wight it does not reach 3m (10 feet). The smallest range in the British Isles centres on the north-east coast of Ireland and south-west Argyle. Here the spring tide range is less than 1·6m (5 feet), while the neaps can be as little as 60cm (2 feet), so that at times the tidal level seems to be more or less unchanged for several days. Obviously, given such striking variations in tidal behaviour, the make-up of shore life differs markedly in different places.

Wave action

If you have ever stood on a headland you will probably have noticed the roughness of the water on the windward side compared with the calmer water lying on its lee or sheltered shore. On rocky shores in particular this is reflected by the variation in number and species of seaweeds and shore animals with the different conditions. Some species tolerate rough water much better than others. For example, the short, tough, sturdy strands of channelled wrack (*Pelvetia canaliculata*) are much better able to cope with the tearing and buffeting action of the water than egg wrack (*Ascophyllum nodosum*), with its large air bladders – an adaptation which provides buoyancy and gives maximum exposure to light for food production at high tide. Such structures are least damaged in calmer water conditions. In the exposed conditions often encountered on headlands even the tenacious barnacles sometimes abandon the bare rock to the sea.

Increased wave action also has the effect of extending the area of shore which can be colonised by living organisms. Thus on westerly coasts vertical cliff-faces are subject to the action of powerful waves brought across the Atlantic. These waves break at a higher point on the cliff-face than in more sheltered bays and the explosion of spray raises the marine influence to higher levels. This is well illustrated by the comparison of Parkmore Point, County Kerry, and Clachan Sound, Argyle, described by J.R. Lewis in his book *The Ecology of Rocky Shores*.

At Parkmore Point the black lichen zone extends to between 6 and 9m (20–30 feet) as compared with less than 1m (2–3 feet) at Clachan Sound. Barnacles and mussels tend to dominate the area covered by the mean spring tide, while the sparse seaweeds of the exposed areas are replaced by luxuriant growths of several species in the calm water that forms Clachan Sound. Finally, in the oarweed zone, dabberlocks (*Alaria esculenta*) is favoured by the strong wave action of the headland, whereas oarweed (*Laminaria digitata*) dominates this region at Clachan Sound.

As the wave action increases the commoner seaweeds of rocky shores disappear in the following order. The first to vanish is egg wrack, followed by bladder wrack, which is often replaced by a form of this seaweed without bladders. The next to go is serrated wrack (*Fucus serratus*) and finally channelled wrack.

Some seaweeds such as sea palm (*Postelsia*), an intertidal seaweed from the Pacific coast of North America, actually thrive on rocky headlands exposed to the full pounding of the surf.

Beach slope

The region of the shore exposed between low and high tide is smaller on a steeply sloping beach than on one with a gentler incline, it therefore provides a much smaller area for colonisation. On shores strewn with large boulders and ridges of rock and on sandy shores of gentle slope, much wave energy is dissipated as the tide comes in, causing limited disturbance and favouring colonisation by beach organisms.

Beach material

Inevitably the life of the shore is affected by the material of which the shore is composed. On rocky shores areas of limestone, such as that at Port St Mary in the Isle of Man, erode to form rich rockpools holding a vast variety of beach animals and plants. The soft chalk of southern cliffs is a suitable material for the establishment of rock boring piddocks (bivalve molluscs), an impossible feat on the hard granite of Cornwall. This does, however, form a stable material for seaweed attachment. The erosion of the chalk by the elements to boulders and pebbles is encouraged by the activities of the piddocks. In contrast, seaweeds blanket the granite rock and protect this already resistant material from the destructive force of the sea. When pebbles are formed they are hurled by the sea against both cliff and rock, creating further erosion and are rapidly reduced in size. Such shingle beaches are frequently disturbed, drain rapidly and experience rapid temperature changes. They are not good places to live as far as the beach organisms are concerned. Thus rocky shores, particularly when associated with pebble and shingle beaches, tend to be sites of active erosion. The coast of Dorset around Durdle Door and Lulworth Cove is typical of such conditions.

In contrast, particles of sand and silt are held apart by the capillary layer of water which surrounds them, preventing much grinding, so that only the roughest wave action has much effect. Sandy and silty shores are associated with deposition rather than erosion, and thus increase in land area (though not volume). They tend to occur in bays and estuaries, and the addition of organic mud and bacteria which inevitably occurs in such areas enriches the relatively stable environment and

encourages colonisation by animals such as lugworms (*Arenicola marina*) well adapted to live in such conditions. The estuaries and bays of the Lancashire and Cumbrian coasts illustrate this well.

Exposure

Having established the pattern of the tides, the action of the sea and the form and material of the land, let us now examine the extent to which the remainder of the physical environment interacts with beach organisms. Collectively this can be referred to as exposure, and includes the effect of wind, sun and rain. Exposure modifies zonation and goes hand in hand with increased desiccation. Sub-littoral seaweeds such as oarweeds, for example, require 98 per cent humidity in order to survive. Intertidal species such as egg wrack can cope with a relative humidity of 83 per cent. Generally speaking, the higher up the beach seaweeds are found the more resistant they are to desiccation. Thus channelled wrack from the top of the beach is much more resistant to desiccation than toothed wrack found in the lower littoral zone (*see* Chapter 2).

Seaweeds on the beach may appear to be dried out until they are lifted up. It can then be seen that the underlying layers are saturated with water, and extended continuous exposure to direct sunlight is required for this to be lost.

Salinity

Intertidal seaweeds and fauna often have to withstand substantial ranges of salinity. The sun and wind, for example, concentrate the water in rockpools, while the rain dilutes it. Intertidal seaweeds are able to cope with a range of from $0 \cdot 2$ to $3 \cdot 0$ times the concentration of salt water. Permanently submerged seaweeds, such as oarweeds, are unable to cope with such extreme conditions and are only able to survive concentrations between $0 \cdot 5$ and $1 \cdot 4$ times that of sea water.

Certain rockpools of the upper shore have

Seaweed zonation seen from oarweed belt, Scarlett Point, Isle of Man.

fresh water draining into them and are therefore permanently brackish. Such pools are favoured by green seaweeds such as sea lettuce (*Ulva lactuca*) and gutweed (*Enteromorpha intestinalis*). In seas where there is a much lower salinity (the Baltic, for example) the plants are consequently reduced in size.

Temperature

Organisms living in the intertidal region of the beach are exposed to extremes of temperature ranging from high temperatures in summer to snow and freezing conditions in winter. Mobile animals can physically migrate and shelter under rocks or in the shade of boulders from such extreme conditions, but seaweeds and immobile animals of rocky shores are not so fortunate. Most littoral species can survive these extremes although sub-littoral forms (i.e. those normally living below low tide mark) usually die. Some evidence suggests that populations of green blanketweed (*Cladophora rupestris*) migrate downshore in response to lower temperatures in winter. This does not mean that they pull up their holdfasts and walk. What happens is that the populations higher up the shore die off and new populations lower down the shore become established and develop.

Light

Light is the fundamental energy source for food manufacture in plants by photosynthesis. It also regulates the behaviour of animals which depend on the plants directly or indirectly for their food. For photosynthesis to take place the light intensity below the water surface must be at least one per cent of that above it. Thus water clarity is of extreme importance to seaweeds, especially those permanently submerged, as light intensity regulates the depths at which the plants can survive. In winter, because of reduced light conditions, at least one species of red seaweed of the genus *Polysiphonia* and the brown seaweed *Scytosiphon lomentaria* move upshore. The characteristic flora of caves is also determined by reduced light conditions and commonly includes a limited range of red seaweeds.

Descriptions of the shore

The terms 'shore' and 'intertidal' are in common usage, but some clarification of their meaning seems necessary. 'Shore' here refers to the area extending from above the extreme low spring tide mark up to where terrestrial vegetation begins.

'Intertidal' refers to the area lying between tidal levels ELWSTL and EHWSTL and is, therefore, a physical definition.

Three further terms – littoral, supra-littoral, and sub-littoral – are defined in a biological context.

Littoral organisms are those plants and animals which require alternating exposure to air and to wetting either by submersion, splash or spray. On exposed coasts organisms such as the small periwinkle and black lichen of the upper littoral zone extend well above extreme high water spring tide level because high energy waves throw sea spray well above it. However, the upper limit of these organisms may correspond to the EHWSTL in sheltered situations. The limit of the littoral zone, then, is regarded as the upper level to which the small periwinkle (*Littorina neritoides*) and the black lichen (*Verrucaria maura*) extend.

The term supra-littoral is reserved for the lowest level of terrestrial vegetation, exemplified by the orange and grey lichens, and the occasional flowering plants growing immediately above the small periwinkle/black lichen zone.

At its lower level the littoral zone extends down to its junction with the sub-littoral zone occurring where the oarweeds begin. Although the upper part of the oarweed belt is uncovered periodically the bulk of its distribution occurs below the ELWSTL.

2 THE ROCKY SHORE

One of my greatest pleasures has always been to take a group of new students or budding naturalists to the shore. Initially, many think that a rocky shore is a mass of smelly brown seaweeds on which you slip on the way for a swim. Over a few days they invariably become enthusiasts, as they realise that there is a whole range of brown seaweeds which they are able to recognise and name. Soon they are eagerly searching for the beautifully patterned red seaweeds and coping with unfamiliar Latin names, enthusiastically locating their

first hermit crab in an apparently empty dog whelk shell, finding a group of beautiful sea anemones with a whole range of colour variations in a nearby rockpool, or learning to identify different kinds of lichens growing on the rocks.

Lichens

As you make your way down the cliffs, the first non-flowering plants you are likely to encounter are the lichens. These organisms have bodies made up from a fungus and single-celled algae. Each gains some advantage from the other, a phenomenon known to biologists as symbiosis. Lichens come in a variety of colours and forms. Some are like a dusting of

Close-up of grey lichens, including the fruticose lichen *Ramilina siliquosa*.

coarse powder on the rock and can be yellow, green, brown, grey, black or white, forming patches or even appearing to be part of the colour on flat rockfaces. Nearer the sea a grey, erect, bushy lichen (experts call them fruticose, which means shrublike) known as *Ramilina siliquosa* is commonly found. Aesthetically it is very pleasing in form and contrasts beautifully with the orange-yellow *Xanthoria parietina*, which characteristically grows as a flattened circular patch with narrow foliose or leaflike fronds radiating from its centre. It also has disc-shaped fruiting bodies located towards the centre of the patch. Another orange-yellow lichen, much more fragmented in appearance than *Xanthoria*, is *Calaplaca parietina*. The absence of common names makes it difficult to remember the names of lichens, but the Latin names do tell something about the plant. *Xanthoria*, for example, derived from the Greek *xanthos* (yellow), is an orange-yellow lichen and *parietina* refers to parietin, a substance which gives a purple colour when immersed in a strong potash (potassium hydroxide) solution.

Dyes

The use of lichens as dyes goes back to the ancient Greeks and Harris tweeds are traditionally dyed with lichen extracts. The popularity of hand-spinning has renewed interest in the use of lichens as natural dyes. Litmus, the dye used by chemists, was originally derived from a lichen but, like most dyes, it is now made synthetically. Lichens are slow growing and, as huge quantities are needed when they are used as a dye source, it is perhaps conservationally desirable to use those available commercially or else make natural dyes from waste products, such as onion skin which gives a good yellow-brown colour according to wool and concentration.

Most of the lichens described above grow within reach of sea spray at high spring tides, but the encrusting black lichen *Verrucaria maura* grows nearer to the sea, just above the seaweeds. When the tide is out this lichen can be seen as a striking black band around the base of sea cliffs, indicating the upper extent of the littoral zone.

Pollution indicators

Perhaps one of the reasons lichens thrive by the sea is the relatively unpolluted air which they encounter there. Indeed, because of their sensitivity to atmospheric pollutants, particularly sulphur dioxide, lichens have been used as indicators of pollution.

Lichens were also used in medicine and one, known as the tree lungwort (*Lobaria pulmonaria*) because of its resemblance to lung tissue, was used in medieval times to treat diseases of the chest. The apothecaries and physicians of the time reasoned that if a plant or animal in the wild looked like a human organ, this was God's way of indicating a cure. This was known as the 'doctrine of signatures'.

Seaweeds

The rocks and boulders of the rocky shore form a stable base to which plants and animals can become attached. The overhangs, crevices and fissures of the rocks provide a moist refuge from drying winds and hot sun and offer suitable places for sedentary animals to live in or to which more mobile forms may retreat. Blanketing layers of seaweed help the animals similarly during low tides and hide them from the ever-hungry eyes of predatory gulls. They also give protection from fish at high tide. In areas where there is calm water the shore is usually covered in seaweed. The upper shore is dotted with rockpools, with a fair carpeting of green seaweeds, and some pools are lined with what appears to be pink 'rock', on which grow small branching tufts of a pink coral-like plant. Both the pink rock and the plants are in fact red seaweeds and the chalk or calcium carbonate stored in their cells is responsible for their appearance. They are known as *Calithamnion* and *Corallina*

Barnacle-encrusted rock surrounded by bladder wrack (*Fucus vesiculosus*) and egg wrack (*Ascophyllum nodosum*).

respectively and have no vernacular names.

The majority of the shore is strewn and festooned with brown seaweeds so that the three principal types of seaweed – green, brown and red – are soon seen. The colours of the seaweeds are due to the pigments in their cells. The green seaweeds have exactly the same pigments as higher plants. The brown and red seaweeds also have green pigment, but it is masked by fucoxanthin in the brown seaweeds and by phycoerythrin and phycocyanin in the reds. Some of these additional pigments are thought to be more efficient at capturing light in low light intensities, enabling red and brown seaweeds to live well below the tide mark in places receiving insufficient light for green seaweeds to survive.

On a visit to the shore it is useful to look first at brown seaweeds. They dominate the beach, the different species forming an overlapping series from the upper shore down to the sea. First there is channelled wrack, then twisted wrack, bladder wrack, egg wrack and finally toothed wrack, which is succeeded by the laminarians or oarweeds.

Fucoids

Channelled wrack (*Pelvetia canaliculata*) is a tough, sturdy seaweed about 10–15cm (4–6 inches) in length with fronds grooved on one side. It grows in pendant tufts from upper shore rockfaces. It stores a lot of oil in its tissues, which is thought to increase its resistance to desiccation. Twisted wrack (*Fucus spiralis*) is up to 10cm (4 inches) longer and if it is held up in the air by its holdfasts, it twists into spirals as it dries. Bladder wrack (*Fucus vesiculosus*) and egg wrack (*Ascophyllum nodosum*) can both be up to 1m (39 inches) in length and the larger plants may represent two or three season's growth. The air bladders of egg wrack grow at intervals along the whole length of the plant body or thallus. They are graded in size and in older specimens can be up to 10cm (4 inches) long. Those of

bladder wrack are arranged in pairs on either side of the midrib of the fronds. In both plants the bladders buoy up the seaweeds during high tides, giving the photosynthetic cells which cover most of the plant maximum exposure to light. The fronds of toothed wrack (*Fucus serratus*) have serrated edges. Like all other fucoids, the tips of the branches are swollen to form receptacles. Dotted on these are tiny flask-shaped structures called conceptacles, in which the reproductive cells are produced. Unlike the other fucoids, toothed wrack has separate male and female plants, and at low tide the male plants can be distinguished by the orange mucilage which

Left Close-up of three lichen species: grey fruticose lichen (*Ramilina siliquosa*); orange foliose lichen (*Xanthoria parietina*); and black encrusting lichen (*Verrucaria maura*).

Below Egg wrack (*Ascophyllum nodosum*) frond and encrusting red seaweed (*Hildenbrantia* spp) growing on quartz rock with encrusting orange sponge (*Myxilla encrustans*).

oozes from the conceptacles. In all fucoids fertilisation of the eggs by sperm takes place in the sea, outside the parent plants. Millions of reproductive cells are produced, which ensures the success of the fertilisation process. They form part of the temporary inshore phytoplankton during spring, when reproduction occurs. The mucilage which coats the surface of these plants helps to retain moisture at low tide.

Oarweeds

Below the fucoids, extending into the sublittoral zone are the oarweeds or laminarias. Oarweeds are larger than the fucoids and can grow to as much as 2–3m (6–10 feet) in length. They are attached to rocks by massive holdfasts and possess thick stalks or stipes which extend into flattened leaf-like laminae or blades. The lamina is dotted by tiny conceptacles in spring from which reproductive

Serrated or toothed wrack (*Fucus serratus*).

material is produced. In common oarweed (*Laminaria digitata*) the lamina is broad and splits into long strap-shaped structures. Sugar kelp (*Laminaria saccharina*) is long and narrow and has an undulating surface. During the Second World War it was used as a source of sugar. The mucilaginous coat of seaweeds is made up of chemicals known as alginates. They are used as emulsifying agents in hundreds of different products nowadays including ice-cream, paints, cosmetics and toothpaste.

Water loss

Since the upper part of the shore is less frequently submerged by the sea than the lower, it is probable that the pattern of seaweed distribution noted above is due to differences in resistance to water loss. Water loss can be investigated using a clothes-line and pegs, three large, tough plastic bags and a 5kg spring balance (marked off at 100g intervals) such as can be obtained at a fishing tackle

shop. Collect 5kg each of toothed, bladder and channelled wrack or other kinds of seaweed in the plastic bags as they are exposed by the falling tide. Peg the weed samples out on the clothes-line, and re-weigh them at half hour intervals. The first hour shows little difference in weight loss between the species, but after three hours the serrated wrack will proportionately weigh less than the channelled wrack. Only water loss can account for this loss in weight. Another method is to soak the seaweeds in buckets of sea water for ten minutes after each weighing, when they are again re-weighed. In this experiment the pegging out period is extended progressively thus: ½, 1, 1½, 2, 3, 4, 5 and 6 hours. At first all species regain weight by water reabsorption. Later in the experiment, first the toothed wrack and then the bladder wrack lose their ability to recover. This demonstrates that lower littoral species are unable to survive the same degree of exposure or dehydration as the upper littoral forms.

To be seen pegging out seaweed on washing lines provokes interesting comments from passing tourists. I am sure they regard us as slightly mad. Young naturalists, however, learn much from the experiments and they can add significantly to the fun of a holiday.

Thongweed *Himanthalia elongata*

This brown seaweed grows abundantly in the mid-lower shore position on more exposed beaches – for example, Port St Mary in the Isle of Man and beaches in South Devon such as Jennycliffe, Plymouth. It begins life as a mass of turgid, shiny, globular structures, yellow ochre to brown in colour, about 2cm tall and 1cm wide at the top, packed tightly together. Each plant develops into a flattened discoid structure about the shape and size of a Pontefract cake on a stalk. Following this fascinating metamorphosis a flattened greeny-

brown thong starts to grow out of the centre of the disc and branches into two at regular intervals. Thongweed is often found with all these stages of development growing close together.

Red seaweeds

The red seaweeds have been sadly neglected, but their range of texture, pattern and colour is a joy to behold. The edges of a midshore rockpool will often yield the delicately veined 'oak leaves' of *Phycodrys rubens* or the oval-leaved *Delesseria sanguinea*, while the thick, tough, leathery purple-red sheets of *Dilsea carnosa* contrast sharply with the delicate lobes of the plants mentioned above. Four other red seaweeds, all of which are edible, are commonly found on rocky shores.

The first of these, red lettuce or laver (*Porphyra umbilicalis*), looks like a thin sheet of translucent pinky-red plastic 10–18cm (4–6 inches) in diameter pinned to the rock at its centre by the holdfast; as the plant ages it may become discoloured, looking brown, green or white in part. Rocks colonised by this plant become very slippery and are best avoided.

Carragheen or Irish moss (*Chondrus crispus*) and batters frond (*Gigartina stellata*) are easily confused, particularly in the immature state. The flattened thalli are 7–20cm (3–8 inches) long and fork at regular intervals. They vary in colour from a translucent brown to a strong purple-red according to where they are growing. They can be found from upper midshore right down to sub-littoral locations, attaining the greatest size and vigour at their lower shore position. When mature, batters frond can be distinguished from the other species by the presence of a dense rash of small pimples protruding from one surface of the thallus, particularly towards the tips of the fronds.

Dulse (*Rhodymenia palmata*) has a flat, translucent red thallus and consists of a main frond from which short, finely stalked, oval-shaped lobes radiate out; in older material this

Opposite Oarweeds at low tide.

Above Brown seaweed – thongweed
(*Himanthalia elongata*) – various stages:
(a) yellow 'bulb' stage; (b) flattened discoid;
(c) mature form with thongs.

Below Herbarium specimen of red seaweed.

pattern may be modified somewhat. The plant is 10–30cm (4–12 inches) long; small specimens are common in midshore rockpools and large ones are characteristically found among the holdfasts of oarweeds on the lower shore.

Red seaweeds with their complex scientific names are perhaps best remembered by making a small herbarium. The natural adhesiveness of the thalli simplifies the job. All that is needed is a pair of scissors, a shallow dish or tray of sea water and some pieces of cartridge paper about the size of a postcard. It is best to take small amounts of plant material and prune away the excess with scissors. Float the seaweed into the water and slip the cartridge paper under it, then spread out the plant with a pair of forceps or tweezers and withdraw the paper and seaweed together from the tray. Allow surplus water to drain away, then keep the specimen lightly pressed until dry. With a little practice and skill preparations can be obtained which look as if they have been painted onto the paper.

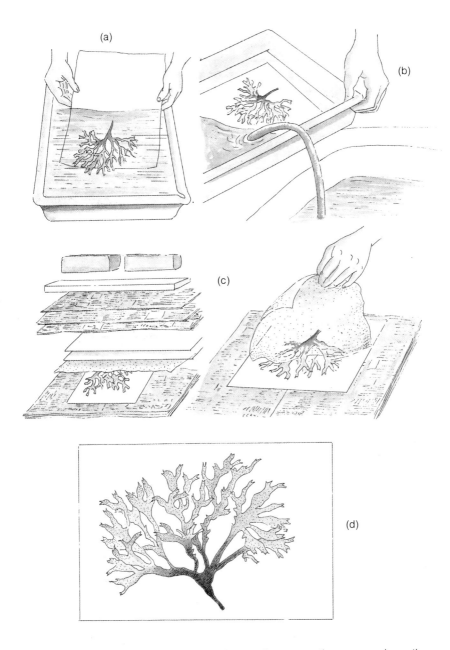

Figure 5 Mounting red seaweeds: (a) float specimen and pass mounting paper underneath; (b) withdraw specimen plus paper carefully or remove water by siphoning off; (c) cover mount with absorbent material such as medical gauze or newspaper and press under weights for a few days; (d) label mounted specimen.

Green seaweeds

Green seaweeds can be similarly collected and preserved – though their brilliant colour often fades, so they are perhaps better left to grow. A westering sun slanting its beams into a shallow, brackish upper shore rockpool crowded with the translucent emerald green tubes of gutweed or the fluted saucer shapes of sea lettuce, their brilliant colour illuminated with light, is one of the most beautiful sights in nature. As you peer deep into the water of lower shore rockpools you can often see the green fronds of *Bryopsis plumosa* looking like a forest of miniature green fir trees.

The beautiful yellow-green seaweed named *Codium* grows in rockpools and can be from 25 to 30cm (10–12 inches) in length. It is pencil thick, of felt-like texture, and branches into two at regular intervals, looking like a small, green shrub.

Animals

Like the plants, the animals of the seashore also show signs of zonation. Parallels can be

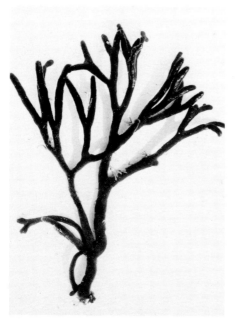

observed in the distribution of acorn barnacles, periwinkles and top shells.

Barnacles

Two main types of barnacles may be found on rocky shores, the encrusting acorn barnacles and those with a distinctive contractile stalk, the goose barnacles. Acorn barnacles are probably the first animals you will encounter on a rocky shore. They are easy to spot since their presence causes a change in the texture and colour of the rock, and they certainly provide a more secure foothold than the slippery seaweeds. Acorn barnacles look very different from the goose barnacles found lower down the shore. Close examination with a hand lens will reveal that a sheet of acorn barnacles is made up of a series of castellated towers, with a series of plates forming a sort of internal roof within the battlements, which provide protection against predators, desiccation and changes in salinity.

The pattern of these plates is used to distinguish two common species, *Balanus balanoides* and *Chthamalus stellatus*. More resistant to desiccation, *Chthamalus* is usually found higher up the shore than *Balanus*. The higher mean sea temperature experienced up to 1960 favoured the spread of *Chthamalus* (with its more southerly distribution) at the expense of *Balanus*. A reverse in mean sea temperature since 1960 has favoured *Balanus*, which shows a preference for colder water conditions. A further species, which became established during the Second World War, is *Eliminius modestus*. Its tolerance of brackish conditions makes it more common in estuaries and harbours. For a fuller consideration of the factors regulating barnacle distribution the book by Roger Brehaut listed in the bibliography is useful.

If you observe a group of barnacles in a rockpool, particularly as the tide is coming in,

Left Green seaweed (*Codium* spp).

Barnacles and a limpet.

or place a stone encrusted with barnacles in a large jar of fresh sea water, you can see the valves open and their hair-fringed legs sweep rhythmically through the water, sieving out the phytoplankton on which they feed. Barnacles in their larval state are part of the zooplankton; but when they reach maturity, they settle on their backs and attach themselves to rocks, leaving their legs free for collecting food. The possession of jointed legs is a clear indication that these animals are crustaceans and not molluscs or shellfish, like the periwinkle.

Goose barnacle *Lepas anatifera*

Goose barnacles have a shell about 5cm (2 inches) long, made up of five bluish-white translucent plates with narrow blackish-brown edges. Between these protrude hairy jointed limbs or cirri which sieve phytoplankton from the sea. The whole of this structure is attached to boats and driftwood by a blackish/olive-brown retractable stalk, which is often up to 15cm (6 inches) long.

Goose barnacles frequently feature in myth and legend. Medieval scientists regarded them as an immature stage in the life-cycle of the barnacle goose, the black stalk of the barnacle resembling the neck of the bird and the black and white limy plates being similar to the body and wings. The presence of the adult goose in winter and not summer in north-west Britain was thus accounted for in the days before the migration pattern of the bird was understood.

Dog whelk *Nucella lapillus*

Patches of acorn barnacles often contain individuals in which the outer wall of fused limy plates is present, but the living contents have disappeared. This leaves what looks like a series of extinct miniature volcanoes. It may be due to natural death, but is much more likely to have been caused by dog whelks, which feed on barnacles. These carnivorous snails can be distinguished from periwinkles

Above Dog whelks (*Nucella lappillus*). The banded form of this predatory snail is said to owe its coloration to an alternating diet of barnacles (white) and mussels (black). The more common white form is also shown.

Below Beadlet anemone (*Actinia equina*) fully extended and just being exposed at low tide. Note the mauve beadlets at the junction of the trunk and tentacles.

by the possession of a siphonal groove. This is a parallel-sided groove located on the rim of the shell opening or aperture and is designed to protect and accommodate a protrusible muscular tube – the siphon, through which the animal draws oxygenated water in order to respire. Dog whelks attack barnacles by inserting their rasp-like tongues (the lingual ribbon) between the protecting plates in order to clean out the flesh inside. If you pick up a dog whelk (usually found on the underhang of a rock at low tide), it may give off a purple fluid. This contains a poison, purpurin. It is unclear whether the snail kills the barnacle with this substance and then eats it, or mechanically forces its tongue between the barnacle's plates, eating it alive. Evidence for chemical breakdown of the plates and soft tissues by dog whelk digestive juices has also been noted.

Dog whelks also feed on mussels. When they feed exclusively first on barnacles then on mussels then on barnacles again, their shells take on a banded appearance. Dog whelks often crowd into crevices on the underside of rocks, where they mate. Internal fertilisation precedes the production of stalked straw-coloured capsules, each about 7mm (¼ inch) in height and found in groups of twenty to thirty. Of the hundreds of eggs within each capsule only a few are fertile. These young feed on the yolk of the unfertilised eggs and in about four months up to a dozen young individuals emerge. They move down the shore away from the adults and migrate back into the barnacle zone when they are about one-third fully grown.

Sponges

In rockpools of the upper shore creamy-grey flattened oval sacs 2–3cm (about 1 inch) long are often found hanging from the red seaweed *Corallina*, either individually or in small groups. They are known as purse sponges. A typical mid to lower shore species is *Grantia compressa*. They filter water through fine

Breadcrumb sponge (*Halichondria panicea*) with encrusting red seaweed (*Calithamnion* spp).

pores in the walls of their vase-like bodies, discharging it through the terminal pore, or ostiole. Special cells in the walls capture the suspended phytoplankton. Lower down the intertidal zone, purse sponges can also be found growing on a rather beautiful feathery red seaweed, *Plumularia elegans*.

At this level of the shore in protected crevices and on the undersides of overhanging rocks draped with seaweeds two other sponges may be found encrusting the rock, each resembling a sheet of tiny volcanoes. One of these, the breadcrumb sponge (*Halichondria panicea*) ranges from creamy-white to green in colour. The second species is another encrusting sponge with its main distribution on the lower shore, *Myxilla incrustans*. This is a bright rusty-orange colour. If a small piece of sponge is broken off and rubbed between the fingers a granular texture is detected. This is due to tiny branched rods of lime or silica which form the skeletons of these animals.

Star sea squirt (*Botrillus schlosseri*).

These small temperate water sponges are related to the much larger tropical species that are sold as bath sponges.

Sea squirts

Another animal which carpets small areas of the underside of boulders, sometimes together with *Myxilla incrustans*, is the star sea squirt (*Botryllus schlosseri*). Embedded in a thin gelatinous layer, from three to twelve individuals are arranged in star-like groups. Water containing food and oxygen is taken in through individual apertures and discharged through a common pore. These animals are very beautiful and range in colour from blue to reddish-green.

Also hanging from the underside of rocks can be found the distended bags of the two-pored common sea squirt (*Ciona intestinalis*). Yellow-green and about 5cm (2 inches) in length, their swollen state readily distinguishes them from the purse sponges. Even slight finger pressure applied to a sea squirt causes a jet of water to be ejected. Curiously,

the outer jacket of these animals is made up in part of cellulose – a substance more commonly associated with plant cells. The tadpole-like larvae of this group of animals provides the clue to their close relationship with vertebrates. These possess a notochord – a flexible spine-like rod. Above it is found a nerve cord, and the clefts in the pharynx or neck region are comparable to the gill slits of a fish.

Sea mats

The final group of animals which attach themselves beneath rocky overhangs of the middle and lower shore are the sea mats, variously called moss animals or Bryozoa. They form many branched tufts up to 8cm (3 inches) long and are sandy or white in colour. Close inspection shows them to be made up of tiny cell-like compartments. Small anemone-like animals with tentacles protrude from these. Unlike anemones and their relatives the hydroids, their tentacles bear rows of fine hairs, or cilia, creating currents which transfer small food particles into the mouth.

Encrusting sea mats such as *Membranipora* are often seen as delicate mat-like layers on the laminae of oarweeds, while horn wrack (*Flustra foliacea*) is a sub-littoral species of sea mat often thrown up on the shore.

Anemones

Probably the animals most characteristic of rockpools are sea anemones. Like their close relatives the jellyfish, they belong to a group of animals known as the Cnidaria or Coelenterates. Typically, they are built from two layers of cells which sandwich a layer of jelly and possess stinging cells.

Anemones adhere to rocks by means of sticky cells on their basal discs and, although they can move, they usually stay in one place for extended periods. Anemones are often seen as a group of dark red blobs of jelly stuck in a rocky crevice at low tide. These are the beadlet anemones (*Actinia equina*), with rings of clear blue spots at the top of the trunk or

column. These beautiful creatures come in a variety of colours, including brown-red, green, yellow-brown and a crimson-strawberry form with large green spots. When expanded they possess about 200 tentacles arranged in six circles. Many sea anemones feed on crustaceans such as shrimps and on small fish, while other species take the smaller members of the zooplankton. The stinging cells grouped in batteries on the tentacles are discharged if touched by the prey, adhering to and injecting poison into its tissues. The tentacles then bend over carrying the paralysed victim to the anemone's open mouth.

Sea anemone feeding

Pieces of paper soaked in an extract of brine shrimp (*Artemia*) will induce the feeding reaction described above, as will glutathione, a substance present in crustacean body fluids. Interesting experiments can also be carried out with rockpool anemones by placing pieces of gelatine impregnated with different concentrations of various amino acids close to the animal. This not only identifies the amino acids to which the anemone will respond, but demonstrates the creature's high sensitivity to low concentrations of these substances and, therefore, to the body fluids of its prey. Anemones can also be made to respond to tuna fish or pieces of meat from picnic sandwiches. The snakelocks anemone (*Anemonia sulcata*), like the beadlet, is about 3cm (1 inch) tall. It is common in shallow midshore rockpools densely colonised with *Corallina*. This animal is usually a beautiful apple-green colour and has tentacles tinged with purple.

Around the holdfasts of the oarweeds on a good low spring tide it is possible to find the beautiful dahlia anemone (*Tealia felina*). About 5cm (2 inches) tall and 10cm (4 inches) across, the column is a patchy red and green, with pieces of broken shell attached to its sticky, warty surface. Extended, the translucent tentacles are seen to be banded in a

Snakelocks anemone (*Anemonia sulcata*).

variety of colours. If the exposed animal is gently prodded it will squirt out water and contract.

In rockpools over most of the shore the white tentacles and orange column of *Sagartia elegans* are a delight to behold. The plumose anemone (*Metridium senile*), with a brown, orange and white column and fine pointed tentacles, looks like a feather duster and is confined to the lower shore.

Deadmen's fingers

Alcyonium digitatum

A low spring tide is always a good time to scramble out over the rocks; peering between the gaps in the huge blocks of stone it is possible to see a variety of animals typical of the lower littoral and sub-littoral regions. A great thrill is to find the tough yellow-pink bodies of another coelenterate, soft coral or deadmen's fingers. Branched and about 15cm (6 inches) long, these translucent miniature anemone-like animals protrude through the tough ground material and are seen to best

effect when illuminated in silhouette. They then look like an opaque layer of decaying flesh, a sight perhaps responsible for the animal's name.

Jellyfish

These are pelagic animals but are often stranded on the shore. Their batteries of stinging cells located on their tentacles can give a painful sting if carelessly handled. They feed by paralysing small fish that have become entangled in the tentacles surrounding the mouth, which receives the prey for digestion in the stomach located in the umbrella-shaped body.

The common jellyfish (*Aurelia aurita*) is up to 25cm (10 inches) in diameter. The body is transparent, but the four pinky-violet horse-shoe-shaped gonads readily identify it.

Siphonophores

The Portuguese man-of-war (*Physalia physalis*) is neither jellyfish nor anemone, but is related to both. It has colonies of stinging hydroids on its tentacles which extend to many feet in length. Its air-filled bag or pneumatophore is

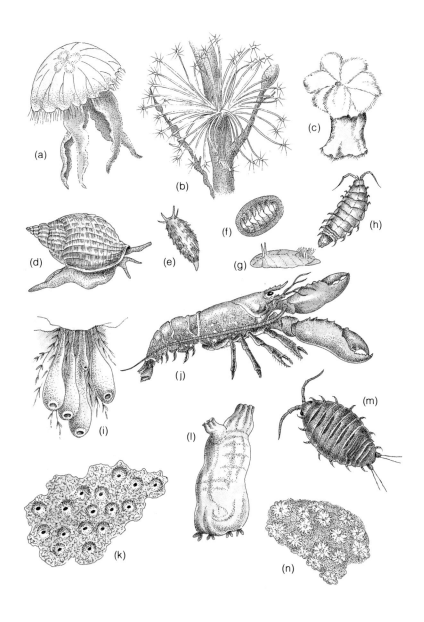

Figure 6 Selected animals of the rocky shore: (a) common or moon jellyfish (*Aurelia aurita*); (b) sea fir (*Clava squamata*); (c) plumose anemone (*Metridium senile*); (d) gastropod showing foot, siphon and tentacles; (e) common sea slug (*Aeolidia papillosa*); (f) coat of mail shell; (g) sea lemon (*Archidoris pseudoargus*); (h) isopod (*Idotea baltica*); (i) purse sponge (*Grantia compressa*); (j) common lobster (*Homarus gammarus*); (k) breadcrumb sponge (*Halichondria panicea*); (l) seasquirt (*Cionia intestinalis*); (m) *Ligia oceanica*; (n) star sea-squirt (Botryllus schlosseri).

pale blue shot with pink and enables the animal to sail before the wind. Groups of these animals are often blown onto our south-west coasts and are dangerous to swimmers, inflicting painful wounds on contact.

Starfish and sea urchins

The lower shore is a favourite hunting ground for two common echinoderms – from the Greek *echino* (spiny) and *dermis* (skin) – namely the starfish and the common sea urchin. Animals of this group are either radially symmetrical with the body plan based on five arms, as in the starfish, or globose as in the sea urchin. In the sea urchins the under-lying five-armed plan can be recognised by the five double rows of tubefeet.

Starfish (*Asterias rubens*) are carnivorous animals feeding by protruding their stomachs, turning them inside out over their prey, or in the case of mussels into the gaping shell, and digesting them alive. The common sea urchin (*Echinus esculentus*) grows to about 10cm (4 inches) in diameter. It possesses a cal-careous skeleton of fused plates directly below the skin. The beautiful pinks and purples which pigment its skin are a joy to behold, but can lead to its undoing, as unscrupulous collectors scrape the spines from the skin, cut around the mouth with a knife and remove the shell contents in order to make ashtrays or even lampshades. The reproductive organs or roe are used as human food (hence the specific name *esculentus*, which means edible), while the five-toothed chewing organ used to browse small plants and animals from rocks is also sometimes collected as an ornament and is known as Aristotle's lantern. The tube feet of rocky shore sea urchins and starfish carry suckers and are used for movement and attach-ment.

Sea urchins are easily dislodged with a stout fishing net and if supported over a wide-mouthed jar of fresh sea water will often dis-charge eggs or sperm into it. This should be done in spring when the animals are ripe.

Common starfish (*Asterias rubens*).

Apart from the thrill of seeing this, provided the sea water is kept cool, the sperm-laden liquid can be mixed with a few eggs in a shallow glass dish. The process of fertilisation can then be observed through a microscope and the early stages of embryonic division witnessed. At Port Erin Bay on the Isle of Man once the inshore trawlers have put in and the tide has fallen, you may pass mysterious rows of sacks on the quayside and, if you listen, you can hear the snapping of the 'queenies' or queen scallops (*Chlamys opercularis*) inside them, waiting for the first stage of their journey to France. As you descend the steps of the stone jetty, the smell of salt and kelp mixed with that of diesel and decay assaults your nostrils and, walking round the moored hulls of the trawlers, if you can successfully compete with the herring gulls, you may be able to collect rejects from the trawl, including other echinoderms such as sunstars, cushion stars and brittle stars.

Ribbon worms

Long unsegmented ribbon worms may also be found among trawl rejects. One of these, the bootlace worm has from six to twelve pairs of eyes, is grey-black in colour and is said to be the longest British animal. Indeed, W.C. McIntosh, the Victorian naturalist, stated that 27·5m (30 yards) of one worm were measured, yet it was only half uncoiled!

Certainly these worms are commonly several feet long, although the commonest, the redline worm (*Lineus ruber*), is only 7 to 14cm (3–6 inches) in length. All these worms are carnivorous and feed on bristle worms, engulfing them like a snake with the aid of a proboscis.

Bristle worms

The more familiar segmented worms are abundant in number and variety on a rocky shore. Although related to earthworms, most marine worms have many well-developed hairs or chaetae and are, therefore, known as polychaetae or bristle worms. Many bristle worms, such as *Sprirorbis*, produce small calcareous tubes and are found growing on toothed wrack; others, such as *Potamoceros triqueter*, are found strung out on stones. From their tubes these worms extend brilliantly

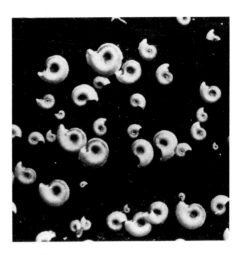

Spirorbis on seaweed.

coloured gills bearing small fine hair-like cilia which, by beating, convey food particles to the worm's mouth.

In contrast, the free-living carnivorous ragworms have well-developed limbs on each body segment that enable them to crawl

Scaleworms (*Harmothoe* spp).

around rocks and to swim with beautiful serpentine movements through mud and sand. Many species range from 12 to 25cm (5–10 inches) in length, while the largest, the king rag (*Nereis virens*), can reach 60cm (2 feet). Their heads possess numerous pairs of eyes and other well-developed sensory organs. They also have a protrusible pharynx which bears fine teeth and prominent jaws with which they grasp their prey. They are found in thin layers of mud and in sand that has accumulated under boulders. Similar places, but towards the lower end of the shore, are the haunt of the less active scaleworms, which have hard, limy overlapping plates protecting their dorsal surfaces. Some of these are carnivorous, often eating other worms.

Another common burrowing worm found in the organically rich debris below the stones on the lower shore is the red thread (*Cirratulus cirratus*). Up to 12cm (5 inches) in length, these worms typically bear thin elongated red-orange threads up to 9·5cm (4 inches) long, which are feeding tentacles and gills. They collect debris from which edible matter is sorted by flaps around the mouth. Thus they avoid the indiscriminate swallowing of

material that occurs in the lugworms of sandy shores.

Periwinkles

No consideration of the rocky shore would be complete without a look at the periwinkles. Four species inhabit the seashore: the small, the rough, the flat and the edible periwinkle. Each has adaptations of structure, physiology and behaviour which relate to the particular ecological niche it occupies. They are all herbivorous and possess a limy door or plate (operculum) to seal off the opening to their shells from predators. They are all fairly rounded, their thickish shells rolling with the sea rather than resisting it.

Small periwinkle *Littorina neritoides*

The range of the small periwinkle extends to the upper extreme of the littoral zone and it is capable of withstanding long periods of desiccation and high temperatures, surviving 49°C for short periods. It is 5mm (⅕ inch) high, feeds on lichens and is an air breather like its neighbour the rough periwinkle. Its fertilised eggs are discharged into the sea and produce planktonic larvae. Its spawning

Some characteristics of four species of periwinkle

Species	English name	Colour range/ Association	Location on shore	Adaptation to wave action	Resistance to desiccation	Respiration	Reproduction
Littorina neritoides	Small periwinkle	Brown–grey to black. Lichens.	Upper littoral zone	Avoided. Out of sea mostly.	Opercular. Rock crevices.	Vascularised mantle cavity, reduced gill.	Liberation of spawn in season coincides at 14 day intervals with spring tides. Long time in larval state.
Littorina rudis	Rough periwinkle	White, yellow, brown, black. Seaweed and rocks.	Upper littoral zone and upper midshore.	Avoided. Lives in crevices.	Opercular. Crevices.	Same as small periwinkle.	Penis/internal fertilisation. Viviparous. Avoids hazards of planktonic existence.
Littorina littoralis	Flat periwinkle	White, yellow, pink, brown, black, green. Seaweed.	Lower middle and upper lower shore.	Avoided. Lives on fucoids; gains protection/ camouflage too.	Opercular. Depends on humidity from alga thalli.	Normal gill.	Eggs laid on seaweeds. Vulnerable to but protected against desiccation, predation and wave action. Avoids planktonic hazards. Does not need to search for home.
Littorina littorea	Edible periwinkle	Brown, black, red. Rocks and seaweed.	HWNT–MLWS	Thickened shell, strong columella. Lives on rocks, sand and mud.	Opercular seal. Mucus membrane also used for attachment.	Normal gill.	Short planktonic existence. Spawns February–April; settles May–June.

habits show a fortnightly rhythm corresponding to the sequence of high tides in spring, the only ones likely to submerge it so as to allow the eggs to be released. When the larvae settle, they appear lower on the shore and adopt a neat strategy to rejoin their parents. Not only do they react against the pull of gravity in that they always move upshore, but they also move away from light when they are dry and towards it when they are wet. So, as the rising tide covers them, they emerge from their dark crevices into the light and the sea carries them up the shore to join the adult population.

Rough periwinkle *Littorina rudis*

The rough periwinkle was for a time reclassified as *L. saxatilis*, but it has now been shown in a paper by Heller that *L. rudis* is a separate species with different breeding habits. The rough periwinkle has a rough textured multi-ridged shell. Like the small periwinkle, it has evolved towards great inde-

Above Flat or smooth periwinkle (*Littorina littoralis*).

Below Ribbon worm (*Lineus ruber*).

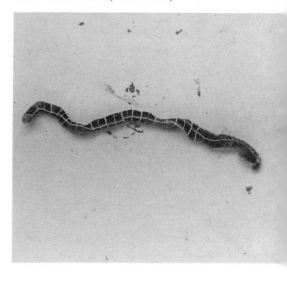

pendence from the sea, particularly in its breeding behaviour, for it relies upon internal fertilisation like all periwinkles, but also practises vivipary (bring forth young as small immature adults), thus avoiding the hazards of planktonic life. Despite this, it lives lower down the shore, typically grazing on channelled wrack.

Flat periwinkle *Littorina littoralis*

The flat periwinkle lacks a spire and at 1cm in height is slightly larger than the rough periwinkle. It has a number of colour forms and, like the edible periwinkle, its range extends throughout the middle shore and it uses gills for gaseous exchange. It shows a preference for grazing on the fronds of toothed wrack and bladder wrack. There is some evidence that particular colour forms are camouflaged from predators against the background of these seaweeds, which also provide protection from desiccation and wave action. These advantages also apply to the strings of jelly-like eggs that are laid on the protective plants.

Edible periwinkle *Littorina littorea*

The edible periwinkle can seal itself by means of mucus onto the rocks as a protection against desiccation. It grazes on seaweeds growing on the rocks. The larvae are discharged into the sea, where they pursue a brief planktonic existence before returning to the midshore region.

Top shells

The top shells are gill breathers and are confined to rocky shores since mud would block their gills. Like the periwinkles they are herbivorous snails, grazing on small seaweeds from rocks on the middle and lower shore. The largest intertidal species and probably the most beautiful is the painted top shell (*Calliostoma zizyphinum*).

Limpets

Limpets are gill-breathing herbivorous snails and are distributed across the mid and lower regions of rocky shores. The largest, the

Top shell (*Calliostoma zizyphinum*) on rocks.

common limpet (*Patella vulgata*) can be 6–8cm (about 3 inches) long and about half as high, and is dome-shaped. This shape combines the greatest adhesion with the lowest water resistance.

The grip of a limpet is proverbial, and they can be dislodged only by a sharp blow. Suction alone is not enough to account for this force, which in three year-old limpets (usually the oldest) is so great that the shell leaves an oval groove in softer rocks. This tight fit protects the animal from desiccation and predators. It also holds water inside the shell and around the gills, facilitating respiration at low tide. The scoring of the rock surface by the shell suggests that the limpet has a permanent base, to which it returns after excursions at high water to graze on seaweeds.

The strength of their homing instinct can be measured by moving limpets to different distances from their bases and noting the minimum distance required to create 'absentees' after the next tide. Shells and locations are marked with cellulose paints of different colours. If you dislodge a limpet to examine it, do so on a rising tide, because even if you replace the animals in their original positions the gulls are likely to reach them before a hold is re-established. Two smaller species, *P. aspera* and *P. depressa*, are more commonly found in the south and west.

The blue rayed limpet (*Patina pellucida*), a limpet of the lower shore, grows to 1·5cm (approximately ½ inch) long. It is found on oarweeds and has a number of iridescent blue lines radiating across the shell.

Chitons (coat of mail shells)

Lepidoplurus asellus

These small grey animals, about 2cm (⅞ inch) long and looking rather like woodlice, are sometimes found in rockpools of the lower shore. Careful removal reveals the muscular foot typical of a mollusc. The segments, which look superficially like those of a crustacean, are a series of calcareous plates.

Chiton or coat of mail shell.

Sea hares *Aplysia punctata*

The mottled brown sea hare is often seen gliding gracefully across a rockpool in search of its favourite food, sea lettuce. This beautiful animal, up to 14cm (5½ inches) long, gets its name from the ear-like appearance of its second pair of tentacles. It is not a true sea slug, as it possesses a hidden shell. When the animal is touched it exudes a purple dye.

Sea lemon *Archidoris pseudoargus*

The sea lemon is a true sea slug in that it has no shell. It has a warty skin, is up to 7cm (3 inches) in length and feeds on encrusting sponges. The sea lemon is a nudibranch, a reference to its external gills. These beautifully coloured feathery structures are seen to their best advantage when expanded in the water.

Common shore crabs (*Carcinus maenas*) pairing.

Mussels *Mytilus edulis*

One of the commonest bivalves of the rocky shore, the mussel has already been mentioned as the prey of the dog whelk and the starfish. Mussels filter suspended food particles from oxygenated water passed over its gills in order to respire. Better adapted for movement in silt and mud, the mussel secures itself on rocks by a series of 'guy ropes' called byssus threads. These can be broken, but are easily renewed so that the mussel can reposition itself. It will be described in greater detail later.

Crustaceans

These are jointed limbed animals with their skeletons on the outsides of their bodies and include barnacles, which have been described above; decapods, isopods and amphipods are considered here.

Decapods

Crabs, lobsters, shrimps and prawns are some of the larger arthropods that inhabit the shore. Because of their calcareous outer skeletons they are known as crustaceans, and the fusion of the head and thorax covered by a carapace makes them decapods. Physiologically, these animals have adapted to widely fluctuating changes in the salinity of the water in which they live, so that they have been able to spread successfully into estuaries and salt marshes where brackish water conditions occur.

Crabs are probably associated more closely with the shore than any other animal except perhaps the starfish. I remember spending many hours as a child fishing for crabs with the fleshed half of a mussel shell suspended from a piece of string through the slats in a wooden pier at Morecambe. Once the crabs got hold they would seldom let go and we would tease them out of their rocky strongholds below. My bucket of sea water was usually soon full of clattering crabs as I competed with other boys to get the best catch.

The two commonest crabs are the shore crab (*Carcinus maenas*), usually green, and the edible crab (*Cancer pagurus*), which is red. Both species are omnivorous scavengers, eating anything dead or alive – with the exception of sea anemones, since they are susceptible to their stings. Porcelain crabs (*Porcellana* spp) differ in that their mouthparts possess fringed hairs which sieve food particles from sea water. Hermit crabs (*Eupagurus* spp) feed in both ways and so have the best of both worlds. On the lower shore spider crabs (characterised by their long legs and claws) are found, as is the lovely *Portunus puber*, clearly a swimming crab with its two pairs of rear limbs flattened and fringed with hair. To distinguish these crabs and the many deep water species occasionally stranded on the shore the key for the non-specialist by J. and M. Crothers listed in the bibliography is extremely helpful.

The shore crab selects his mate a few days before she moults and carries her beneath him. Once moulting occurs he turns her over so that their ventral surfaces are in contact and copulates with her while her skeleton is still soft. In south-west Britain this occurs between July and September. Females appear between January and April with collections of eggs (egg plugs) attached to their undersurfaces. They are then known as 'berried females'. Both salinity and temperature have been shown to affect the breeding cycle of the shore crab. Eggs can develop normally at 10°C, but only at salinities above 26 per cent. At lower temperatures even higher salinities are required for breeding success. Declining autumn temperatures are thought to stimulate fertile females to migrate offshore to the safety of a more consistent saline environment. The eggs hatch to planktonic larvae from April to July and settlement of the young crabs occurs

Hermit crab with soft part of body exposed.

in July and August. Variations on this pattern exist, the cycle taking longer in the colder waters of the north.

Unlike the red specimens that grace the table, the common lobster (*Homarus gammarus*) is a beautiful blue colour when alive. It is a crustacean of the deep water so that only rarely are specimens found on the shore. If encountered they should be treated with care as their large pincers can inflict painful wounds.

Squat lobsters are neither lobsters nor crabs, their nearest relatives being the hermit crab. Their carapaces, or shells, are long and narrow like a lobster's while their tails or abdomina are tucked below like a crab's. The claws are about one and a half times the body length, which is up to 12cm (5 inches) long. *Galathea strigosa* is a beautiful red and blue colour and can be found under stones on the lower shore.

Shrimps and prawns are discussed in detail in the chapter on sandy shores (Chapter 3). The old adage 'shrimps on sand and prawns on rocks' reminds us that prawns love the weedy pools of rocky shores and feed avidly on any waste organic matter they encounter. They are also favourite food items for many birds and fish.

Isopods and amphipods

These are two other groups of crustaceans commonly found between the tides, both lacking carapaces. Isopods look like woodlice, are flattened dorso-ventrally and have limbs of equal length. The sea slater (*Ligia oceanica*) is up to 2·5cm (1 inch) long, with antennae two thirds of this length. It is found in crevices among the grey and orange lichens of the supra-littoral zone and is particularly active at night. *Idotea baltica* is another isopod common in rockpools among seaweeds on the lower shore. Its body is much narrower than that of the sea slater and the tip of its tail segment, which is much longer than the others, is formed into three lobes at the free end. The males are up to 3cm in length

(1¼ inches), the females slightly smaller at two-thirds of this.

Amphipods are flattened from side to side. *Gammarus* is sometimes found in rockpools, while the sand hopper (*Talitrus saltator*) is found in rotting seaweed. They are both common on sandy shores.

Fish

A wide variety of inshore fishes (usually smaller examples of species) are found in rockpools. Some, like the sand eel (*Ammodytes tobianus*) and the weever fish (*Trachinus vipera*) are more commonly associated with sandy bottoms, while the eel (*Anguilla anguilla*) and the grey mullet (*Chelon labrosus*) are usually present only as young fish. Weever fish are notorious for the venom-laden spines carried on their dorsal fin and gill cover and have inflicted many painful and inflamed wounds on the hands of sea anglers and on the feet of paddlers. The word 'weever' is related to 'viper' and is reflected in the fish's specific name. Because of the occasional presence of weever fish in rockpools, it is less risky to search for rockpool fish with a pond net rather than with unprotected hands.

Fish such as gobies, sticklebacks and blennies are important food items for economically valuable fish such as cod, salmon and plaice. Others, such as the sea scorpion and particularly the sand eel, are now harvested from the sea to make protein-rich fish meal for the pet food trade. The scale of this business combined with the indiscriminate removal of immature as well as adult fish in fine-gauged nets is currently causing concern among ornithologists and the more enlightened members of the fishing industry, as it could easily lead to the exhaustion of fish stocks that are also an important food source for sea birds such as puffins, shags and gannets.

Many shore and rockpool fish feed on small crustaceans such as sandhoppers and shrimps. In addition, fish like blennies (*Blennius* spp) take acorn barnacles, as do the beautiful

Butterfish (*Pholis gunellus*) from above.

wrasse, although wrasse (*Labrus* spp) also have a liking for chitons and scaleworms. In contrast, the sand eel and pipefish (*Syngnathus acus*) feed on zooplankton and form a valuable link in the food web of the rocky shore. Many of the sea fish come into shallow water to breed and the eggs and fry can often be found in rockpools of the lower shore. These are sought after as food by other fish. In some fish, such as the goby (*Gobins minutus*), eggs are guarded by the male until hatching is completed.

This protective instinct is perhaps more highly developed in other kinds of fish such as the sea or fifteen-spined stickleback (*Spinachia spinachia*), which, like its more familiar three-spined cousin, builds a nest – in this case made from fragments of seaweed. However, the careful protection of eggs is probably best exemplified by the pipefish. In this species the eggs are passed from the female to the male's brood pouch, where they are fertilised and then incubated for four weeks until they hatch and escape as miniature versions of the adult.

To maintain station in order to guard their eggs many rockpool fish have pelvic fins that are structurally modified to form sucker-like organs by which they attach themselves to rocks. In the goby this merely involves the fusion of the pelvic fins to form a fan-like organ on the underside of the body. However, this development is much more extreme in the case of the sea snail (*Liparis montagui*), a fish despite its name, and the lumpsucker (*Cyclopterus lumpus*). In his book *The Sea Shore* C.M. Yonge describes a lumpsucker which attached itself so firmly to the bottom of a bucket that when taken by the tail, the fish, the bucket and some gallons of water were raised without breaking the suction.

Birds

Gulls

The herring gull (*Larus argentatus*) is found on muddy, sandy and rocky coasts. Indeed a visit to the coast would seem very strange if the mournful cry of the herring gull were missing. This bird has a natural ability to exploit many foods, taking live fish, carrion offal, shrimps, crabs and molluscs. I wonder how many people walking on a beach have been startled by the smack of a mussel being dropped from on high by a gull in order to smash its shell. However, the herring gull probably owes its success to its ability to live with man and to exploit his waste materials. A testimony to this is the spread of the herring gull on the South Walney reserve in Cumbria since the waste disposal dump was established there in the late 1950s. Together with its close relative the lesser black-backed gull (*Larus fuscus*) it dominates the area and has ousted the less aggressive black-headed gull (*Larus ridibundus*) which previously nested there.

Turnstone *Arenaria interpres*

Perhaps more specifically associated with rocky and sandy shores is the turnstone. At 23cm (9 inches) in length this beautiful wader has a bright orange-brown back and a thick black band across its breast, contrasting nicely with its white underparts and striking orange legs. It searches through rafts of seaweed and mussel beds at low water, flicking material over with its short, pointed beak, and takes a range of molluscs and crustaceans, including periwinkles and shore crabs. It does not breed in Britain.

Another migrant wader that winters on our coasts is the purple sandpiper (*Calidris maritima*), which occupies a similar habitat to the turnstone. The oystercatcher (*Haematopus ostralegus*) with its black and white plumage and long red bill is always a welcome sight on a rocky shore. It is commonly found on mud-flats and sandy shores too, and is described in Chapter 4.

In our sophisticated modern cities perhaps little thought is given to the ways in which the plants and animals of the seashore can be used by man. Mention has already been made of periwinkles as food, lichens as dyes and seaweeds as the source of alginates, the emulsifying agents with such a variety of uses. The modern organic gardener improves the humus content of his soil and benefits from the rich mineral content of seaweeds, whether by composting them or applying them as a moisture-preserving mulch to the surface of the soil. The high mineral content of seaweed is further reflected by the early nineteenth century practice of burning kelp, first as a source of soda and potash for soap-making and later in the commercial production of iodine. Cheaper alternative supplies have now made these practices obsolete.

A surprising variety of seaweeds can be used as food. All seaweed used for this purpose needs to be thoroughly washed to remove sand and silt, but once this is done the possibilities are considerable. Care should, however, be taken not to collect material from polluted areas.

3 THE SANDY SHORE

At first glance the sandy shore is strikingly different from the rocky shore. On some beaches in Devon and Cornwall and in certain parts of the Isle of Man the contrast is immediate, because tongues of rocky shore extend into the undulating plain of sand. Sandy shores are not as barren as they sometimes look and an examination of the strand line proves this to be the case.

The strand line, West Eriskay, Outer Hebrides.

The strand line

The strand line is usually marked by a band of material deposited by the last high tide. When the high tide levels have been declining for the previous week, there may be a successive series of such deposits. If you examine this material, you may find grass, wood and leaves, especially if the beach is near an estuary. As the material is turned over, masses of sandhoppers will emerge. These small crustaceans are described in detail below.

As you walk along the strand line, turn

Cases of sand mason (*Lanice conchilega*).

over the litter and collect samples of whatever you find. On a rich beach the number and variety of shells is amazing. There will be molluscs, including bivalves such as clams, cockles, razor shells, yellow and brown tellins, banded wedge, Venus shells and the delicate and beautiful netted architecture of the piddock shell. Univalves will include whelks, tower shells, common wendletraps, the necklace shell and, if you are lucky, the pelican's foot shell. You may find the sand tubes constructed by the sand mason and the delicate cones of the common trumpet worm. Sometimes the remains of masked crabs and potato urchins can also be found.

These are the remains of intertidal species of animals. They have come from within the sand, below its surface, and probably from the very beach on which you are standing. The broad, undulating sandy desert is actually teeming with life – but it is hidden below the surface.

A poor beach will yield very little – perhaps the odd mussel or dog whelk shell from the nearby rocks, occasional fronds of seaweeds, or a few barnacles encrusting part of a fisherman's discarded net.

Life under the sand

Sand-dwelling organisms have a tremendous advantage over the animals of a rocky shore, which cling to the rocks or the seaweeds growing on them and are relatively exposed to the ravages of the elements, predators, or both.

When the tide is in, animals on a sandy shore can either partially emerge from the sand or at least come close to the surface to feed. When the tide is out, they retreat below the surface, remaining moist and protected from predators. Why are some sandy beaches richer in animal life than others? A beach may be affected by a local source of pollution, though this is unlikely to kill off all the animals. Drainage of significant amounts of fresh water into the area can damage some animals, but others, such as the Baltic tellin (*Macoma baltica*), show a preference for brackish conditions and tend to be present in increased numbers.

Of fundamental importance is the size of the sand particles that make up the beach. If the particles are large, the sand is quick-draining and the total amount of water held in the sand by surface tension around the particles is much less than on beaches with fine sand containing a high proportion of silt. Beaches of coarse sand therefore tend to dry out quickly and animals attempting to colonise such areas are liable to suffer from dehydration. Beaches of fine sand and silt drain more slowly; because of the small particle size, water is held more strongly around the particles and the risk of dehydration is less.

In addition, beaches of fine sand and silt are often near estuaries and contain a higher proportion of organic matter. The small particle size means that there is an increased surface area for diatoms to colonise, while bacteria actively feed on the organic material. As both diatoms and bacteria are thought to be a major food source for invertebrates of the sandy shore, all these factors tend to promote an increase in the number and variety of larger beach organisms higher up the food chain.

Plants

While the rocky shore provides a firm base for the anchoring holdfasts of fucoids and oarweeds, on the sandy shore the rock is itself made up of hundreds of tiny sand grains, which are easily disturbed by the water movements. Obviously this surface is unstable and quite unsuitable as a base for these seaweeds. However, that does not mean that there are no plants; it is simply a question of size. The tiny diatoms which grow on or among the sand grains are present in enormous numbers.

In spring, if you catch the light correctly, the surface of the sand looks yellow-green in colour – an indication of the density of the diatoms growing there.

Invertebrate animals

A walk from the high to the low water mark can be very revealing. Wading birds have favourite feeding areas, which can be discovered either directly through binoculars or else by examining patches of sand where their footmarks and small holes made by their beaks provide a clear indication of the presence of the small animals which make up their food. These include lugworms (*Arenicola* spp), whose presence is indicated by saucer-like depressions of up to 5cm (2 inches) across, each with a wormcast 15cm (6 inches) or so away from it. Fishermen who dig lugworms for bait quickly learn to recognise these signs.

Probably the most dramatic evidence of the presence of animals on a sandy shore is the abrupt appearance of jets of water suddenly springing 1·5m (5 feet) or so up out of the sand near the low water mark left by a spring tide. This remarkable phenomenon is caused by the sudden contraction of the powerful muscles of razor shells (*Ensis* and *Solen* spp), which live in vertical burrows just below the surface. Disturbed by the vibration in the sand caused by footsteps, they swiftly bury themselves deeper and hide from danger.

Finally, it is, of course, possible to observe animals directly on the beach. Most readers have probably seen the sudden movement of ghost-like shrimps and prawns in small surface pools. Where there is some sand erosion caused by the flooding or emptying of drainage channels, a chance sighting of a temporarily exposed cockle or tellin is always possible. Here too one can detect the rapid, undulating movements of tiny dabs making themselves almost invisible as they scurry into a cloud of sand. I have also found the upright cases of sand mason worms in the sand of the lower shore, although they have always appeared to be empty – but if you dig with a bait fork, you will find the worms at the base of the tubes.

Surveying a beach

The most scientific way of establishing which animals are present in a beach is to carry out a transect. Using the criteria given above, select a beach that seems to be fairly rich – and, if possible, try to do the work on a good spring tide. Pick a reasonably steep beach, since the distance between the high and low water marks left by a spring tide may be two or three miles on a very shallow beach.

A transect is a measured line extending over the whole or part of the tidal range. Samples of beach material, usually of one square metre and one and a half spade's depth, are taken at regular intervals (say fifty metres) and transferred to a sand box – a stout wooden box with rope handles and a copper-gauze bottom. It is important to dig quickly in order to maximise the catch, as certain animals (for example, razor shells) can burrow very rapidly. The sand box is then carried to the edge of the sea and rocked on its convex base. The sea rapidly washes away the sand, leaving all the organisms living in it trapped on the copper gauze mesh.

This procedure is hard work; it is best carried out by a team of enthusiasts and makes an interesting project for school children or for a natural history group. The workload is eased if you start the transect operation at high tide and follow the falling tide down the shore. It is important not to put too much sand in the box at once; three or four spadefuls are sufficient. This helps to avoid damaging the specimens. The trapped animals are transferred into clearly labelled wide-necked jars of sea water or stout plastic bags of moist seaweed as soon as possible, taking care not to damage them and ensuring that all the catch is removed before taking the next sample. Crabs should be kept separate – otherwise they may consume or damage some of the catch. Once

you have sampled the whole of the square metre, try to keep the animals out of the sun, since exposure to sun raises their body temperature, starves them of oxygen and leads to their death. Using this method, it is possible to get some idea of the numbers of different animal species living below the surface of the sandy shore and their relative distribution across it.

If you have not got a sand box, the sand from the sample site can be piled onto a large plastic sheet and the animals extracted by a team using flour sieves. Two teams of about a dozen people can do this, although it requires careful organisation, and with each team of twelve working alternate sampling sites down the transect line good results can be obtained. It can also be great fun.

Specimens can be identified by reference to books listed in the bibliography. Collins' *Pocket Guide to the Sea Shore* by John Barrett and C.M. Yonge is particularly useful.

Environmental constraints

As we have seen, the animals usually live below the surface of the sand, particularly when it is exposed at low tide. This affords them protection from predators and from dehydration. Other physical constraints which may be critical on a rocky shore are also alleviated on a sandy shore. For example, although sand may be very hot at the surface on a bright, sunny day, the temperature falls quickly with depth, and 15cm (6 inches) below the surface the sand may be 7°C cooler. Temperature changes are therefore not usually a problem, although oxygen availability is reduced when the surface of the sand actually freezes. On beaches full of decaying organic matter the formation of an organically-rich oxygen deficient black sulphide layer a few centimetres below the surface can create respiratory problems, but these are overcome by the various strategies and adaptations described below.

Salinity in a sandy beach tends to remain

Tubes of sand mason (*Lanice conchilega*).

fairly constant. Rain-water falling on such a beach floats on top of the denser saline water below and little mixing appears to take place within the sand, so the sudden changes of salinity which could be disastrous for marine and littoral organisms are usually prevented. Fresh water seepage, however, can lower salinity, producing the brackish areas often favoured by the ragworm (*Nereis diversicolor*). Sand dwelling animals display many structural and physiological adaptations, particularly in relation to building homes in the sand, feeding and obtaining an adequate supply of oxygen.

Worms

Worms of the rocky shore which live in calcareous tubes moulded to either seaweed or stones have already been described (in Chapter 2). Tube-building worms can also be found on the sandy shore. These creatures use locally available building materials such as sand and shell fragments, cementing them together with mucus produced by a gland in the worm's mouth. Two such worms are the trumpet worm and the sand mason.

Trumpet worm *Pectinaria koreni*

The fragile, rather narrow, conical tube of the trumpet worm, is made up of sand grains delicately fixed face to face so as to form a smooth wall. The narrow end of the tube projects upwards through the sand at an angle and the worm lies upside-down within it and discharges sand through the apex. This creates a further vertical shaft to the surface, through which it obtains the organically rich debris on which it feeds. It draws a current of oxygenated water over its gills through the tip of the tube when it is not burrowing, and moves its home when the local food supply is exhausted.

Sand mason *Lanice conchilega*

The sand mason's tube of shell fragments and sand grains can be up to 30cm (1 foot) in length, 3–4cm (2½ inches) of which projects above the surface of the sand. The greater security of this larger tube provides a retreat for the worm in the presence of predators at low tide and compensates for its lack of mobility. This beautifully coloured worm feeds on detritus and when the tide is in the animal's fine feeding tentacles pick up detritus from the adjacent sand surface. The red gills, rich in haemoglobin, are also protruded for respiration. Fine bristles are found on some of the body segments, enabling the worm to move up and down the tube.

Lugworm *Arenicola marina*

The common lugworm, probably the best known worm of the shore, lives in a U-shaped burrow below the sand. A good specimen is 20–25cm (8–10 inches) in length and has a body as thick as your finger. Because of their different feeding methods, lugworms lack the fine mouth tentacles of the sand mason. The saucer-like depression, often with a hole in the

middle, at the head end of its burrow is caused by the worm swallowing large quantities of sand. This is rich in organic matter on the slightly muddy shores favoured by the worm. The organic matter is digested and the sand is ejected as a wormcast through the tailshaft. The walls of the burrow are cemented into place by mucus from the worm's mouth, and it can move to and fro through the burrow or hold itself in a fixed position by means of the fine bristles on the front part of its body. The middle part of the body bears finely branched gills which are well served by blood vessels. The red blood is rich in haemoglobin and is efficient at absorbing oxygen – important for the survival of an animal which often lives in oxygen-deficient conditions. Water is passed over the gills by undulating movements of the animal's body. The tail region is narrower than the rest and makes up the remaining third of the body.

Sea mouse *Aphrodite aculeata*

The sea mouse is a beautiful scale worm, fat and up to 15cm (6 inches) long. It is strictly sub-littoral but is often cast up on sandy shores. Its back and sides are covered in a dense felt of hairs, some of which flash with iridescent colours. This alluring appearance is

Sea mouse (*Aphrodite aculeata*).

perhaps responsible for the worm's somewhat exotic name, *Aphrodite*. Only when the underside is examined does the segmentation which characterises worms become apparent. The sea mouse is related to the carnivorous ragworms which, though more common on the rocky shore, are also found low down on sandy beaches, among sand, grit and gravel.

Crustaceans

Crustaceans are found in abundance on sandy shores. Some, known as amphipods, are flattened from side to side. One of these, the sandhopper (*Talitrus saltator*), is commonly associated with the top of the beach. The density of these animals at dusk is often so great that the sand seems to move under one's feet and their activity gives rise to a persistent rustling sound. At a distance they look like a misty band running along the top of the shore. Sandhoppers grow up to 16mm (³/₅ inch) in length and feed on fragments of plant material. They burrow in the sand or hide under moisture-conserving litter during the day and tend to avoid being submerged by the sea.

Another group of amphipods which thrive when they can burrow in the sand are the haustorids. These include animals without common names, such as *Bathyporeia pelagica* 6mm (¼ inch) long and *Haustorius arenarius* 10mm (²/₅ inch) in length. They feed on vegetable debris and in turn are fed on by shore fish. Like the sandhoppers, they are also an important food source for shore birds. Another of the small amphipods is *Gammarus*, 14mm (½ inch) long. Three common species exist, which look very similar but are physiologically distinct, being adapted to fresh water (*Gammarus pulex*), brackish water (*Gammarus zaddachi*) and marine conditions (*Gammarus locusta*). All three may be encountered on sandy shores near large estuaries.

These physiological differences depend on osmosis. The body fluids of animals living in fresh water contain dissolved materials which are more concentrated than the surrounding water, because by the process of osmosis the semi-permeable membranes protecting the body tissues of these animals allow water to pass inwards but prevent the dissolved substances passing out. These animals have special organs similar to our kidneys which regulate the concentration of their body fluids, removing excess water to the outside of the animal in order to prevent it swelling like a balloon and bursting. Thus, the 'kidney' of *Gammarus pulex* is adapted to deal with fresh water conditions. In brackish or marine conditions the solutions in the surrounding water would be more concentrated than the animal's body fluids, so that the osmotic process would be reversed and water would be removed from its tissues. As a result the animal would quickly become dehydrated and would die.

The other two species are adapted to brackish and marine conditions respectively and the regulation of their body fluid concentrations is adjusted accordingly. Thus each species has become physiologically adapted to a particular set of external conditions.

Large crustaceans

The shrimp (*Crangon vulgaris*), the shore crab (*Carcinus maenas*) and the masked crab (*Corystes cassivellaunus*) are larger crustaceans found on the sandy shore.

The shrimp is adapted to a wide range of salinity and temperature and is at home both on sandy shores and in estuaries. Either buried in the sand or motionless in a pool, it is hardly visible because its pigment cells adjust its colour to that of the background; only movement gives it away. It is omnivorous, feeding on plant and animal material, even taking ragworms larger than itself. It is distinguished from its relative the prawn in that it lacks the sharp spine or rostrum which extends between the eyes of the prawn.

To sample shrimp populations and the sublittoral community generally it is worth using

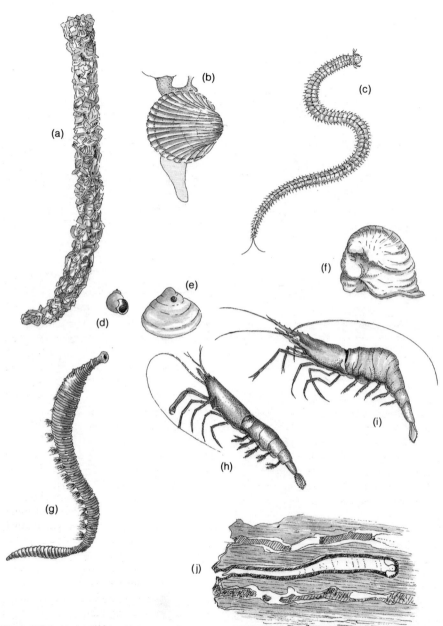

Figure 7 Selected animals found on sandy shores: (a) case of sand mason (*Lanice cochilega*); (b) common cockle (*Cerastoderma edula*); (c) ragworm (*Nereis* spp); (d) necklace shell (*Natica* spp); (e) tellin shell with hole bored through it by necklace shell; (f) slipper limpets (*Crepidula fornicata*); (g) lugworm (*Arenicola marina*); (h) common shrimp (*Cragnon vulgaris*); (i) common prawn (*Leander serratus*); (j) shipworms (*Teredo navalis*).

Sand mason worm removed from case. At low tide, the worm moves to the bottom end of the case and is difficult to locate. Note the sticky filaments or feeding tentacles around the head.

a push net. A pair of thigh boots are also necessary, since working barefoot there is the risk of being stung by a weever fish. Autumn is a good time of year to take a sample, particularly on a good spring tide. At waist depth in the water the net is pushed along and samples are taken by lifting the net clear of the water at about 20m (65 feet) intervals. Push nets usually have a 1·5m (5 feet) leader board which is held at right angles to a 2·5m (8 feet) pole (socketed into the board) which holds the board on the bottom, allowing the net to stream behind. It is a rewarding exercise, for in addition to shrimps a variety of crabs, sea gooseberries, starfish, sea mice and a whole range of fish are trapped. Shrimping at dusk one autumn, I noticed that the water flashed with light whenever the push net broke the surface. This was due to the dinoflagellate *Noctiluca*, which phosphoresces, giving off light when the water is disturbed.

The shore crab appears both on rocky and sandy shores and is described in Chapter 2. The masked crab, however, inhabits the lower shore and the sub-littoral zone. It is typically found buried in clean sand, where its long, hair-fringed antennae interlock to form a fine sand-free tube down which respiratory water currents flow to the gills. At night, when the risk of capture by predatory fish is reduced, it emerges to forage for food and reverses the direction of the current flow over its gills, unclogging sand grains from its antennae. The animal gets its name from the mask-like appearance of its carapace, which can be examined when, as often happens, dead crabs are cast up on the beach.

Molluscs

On sandy and muddy shores bivalve molluscs (those with hinged twin shells) are found in a wide range of shapes, sizes and colours, and display a variety of feeding techniques. Probably the best known is the common cockle.

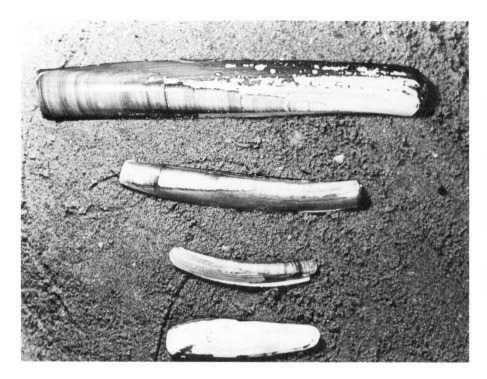

Four different razor shells: **left to right** *Ensis siliqua*, *Ensis arcuata*, *Ensis ensis* and *Pharus legumen*. All these molluscs are suspension feeders.

Suspension feeders

Distributed between the middle and the low tide mark, these animals are present in enormous numbers and are quite easy to find. Cockles (*Cerastoderma edule*) can be brought quickly to the surface if you disturb the sand with your feet. If you put a few in a tray of sea water or jam jar and sit quietly, the valves soon open and out comes the large orange-yellow foot followed by two greyish-white tubes called siphons. If you drop a little fine silt into the water, you will see the lower tube drawing water in and the upper tube expelling it. Razor shells (*Ensis* spp), Venus shells (*Venus* spp) and trough shells (*Mactra* spp) are other suspension feeders, sifting plankton and other fine food particles from the current of water which oxygenates their gills. The rather bulky sub-spherical cockle shell requires a powerful foot to drag it through the sand. The Venus shell, although ridged, is somewhat slimmer, as are the trough shells, making burial in the sand an easier task.

Detritus feeders

Members of the other groups of bivalves found in the sandy shore are comparatively slim and are well adapted for rapid movement through the sand. They include the tellin and the banded wedge shell. These bivalves are deposit or detritus feeders. Like the cockle group they have two siphons, but those of detritus feeders are separated and much larger. The inhalant siphon, like the tube of a vacuum cleaner, sucks up organic debris and bottom-living diatoms.

Three species of tellin are common. *Tellina tenuis* comes in a beautiful range of colours, from pink through yellow or orange to brown. It is found from HWNTL, reaching a maximum density at LWSTL. The empty shells of a second species, *Tellina fabula*, are often found in beach litter, bleached white with beautiful striations over the surface of the right-hand valve. The third species, *Macoma baltica*, prefers brackish conditions. It has a larger and thicker shell than the common tellin and is frequently found in and near estuaries. The shell of the banded wedge shell (*Donax vittatus*) has a beautiful milled edge. The inside is often coloured violet but may be yellow or brown.

Necklace shells *Natica* spp

Empty bivalve shells are often found with one valve perforated by a cone-shaped depression. These holes are 'drilled' by necklace shells in order to feed on them. The common necklace shell (*Natica alderi*) is a carnivorous snail, globular in shape and buff in colour, with a large aperture and a short spire decorated with an iridescent band of blue, green and pink which makes it quite distinct from periwinkles. An additional distinguishing feature is the hole or umbilicus which perforates the columella, the structure around which the shell is formed. The books by N. Tebble and by N. McMillan listed in the bibliography will be of help in identifying the many other species of *Natica*.

Piddocks *Barnea* spp

These bivalves use the fine teeth arranged on the outside of their surprisingly fragile shells to bore into a variety of materials, including chalk, peat, wood, clay and sand. They inhabit an area ranging from the middle shore to the sub-littoral zone. Along with the shipworms (*Teredinidae*), which caused great problems in the days of wooden ships, they are our best known boring molluscs.

Echinoderms

Starfish and sea urchins also colonise sandy

White piddock (*Barnea candida*). This bivalve mollusc can bore into peat, wood, chalk, clay and sand. It is widely distributed and found in the mid-intertidal zone.

shores, but as might be expected they have become adapted to this environment and are, therefore, structurally different in certain respects from their cousins of the rocky shore.

Starfish *Asteropecten irregularis*

About 12cm (5 inches) in diameter, this starfish is flattened in appearance and has five arms each fringed with a row of fine spines. They live in the sand below the low water mark left by spring tides, but may be found higher up the shore after storms. They are carnivorous, feeding on molluscs, crustaceans and worms, and occasionally prey on other echinoderms. The prey is ingested whole, the soft parts being digested and the hard parts disgorged. Their burrows lack a passage to the surface. However, a respiratory current is maintained by the vibration of their pointed tube feet, which are also used for digging.

Sea potato *Echinocardium cordatum*

These widely occurring animals are of midshore to sub-littoral distribution. Sub-

The common sea potato (*Echinocardium cordatum*); collection with spines rubbed off. Found on the middle and lower shore, it burrows to a depth of 7·5cm (3 inches).

globular in shape the average sea potato is about 5cm (2 inches) in diameter and 3·5 cm (1½ inches) deep. They live in burrows up to 15cm (6 inches) below the surface and maintain contact with the surface by a channel through the sand, the walls of which are consolidated by mucus. These animals burrow by using their spines, and water currents from the surface are created which flow over their bodies. This brings a flow of dissolved oxygen over those of their tube feet which act as gills. Other tube feet are very long and extend to the surface. These bear tiny finger-like processes at their tips which pick up food particles deposited on the sand.

Birds

Birds typical of the sandy shore in summer include the cormorant, oystercatcher, curlew, redshank and ringed plover, and a variety of gulls. These are discussed elsewhere in this book.

In winter the variety and number of birds is increased as overwintering migrants throng the shore to take advantage of the rich invertebrate food source. They include the bar-tailed godwit, knot, sanderling, dunlin and grey plover.

Bar-tailed godwit *Limosa lapponica*

At 38–41cm (15–16 inches), these birds are slightly smaller than the curlew but their long, slightly upturned bills and stilt-like legs help to distinguish them. They wade deeply, often completely submerging their heads so as to totally bury their bills in the sand in search of lugworms. Although they occur in small flocks, the British winter population is around 50,000. Of these, 7,000 are located in the estuary of the River Lune at Morecambe Bay, where they arrive around late July and stay until they return to their breeding grounds in late March to early April.

Knot *Calidris canutus*

At 25cm (10 inches) in length the knot is the largest of the small waders and it is often its size which distinguishes it from its common shore companions, the sanderling and dunlin. In winter when the massed flocks are in flight they provide a dramatic spectacle as they twist and turn in unison, first the grey upperparts then the light underparts showing. In late spring their more colourful breeding plumage is of reddish underparts and dark brown back and wings.

They feed on shore crabs, Baltic tellins, sandhoppers, and other crustaceans and this diet fattens the birds ready for their breeding migration to Iceland in early May. Ringing investigations have shown them to have a pre-migration weight of 200–210g (7–7½ ounces); but on their arrival in Iceland they weigh only 150–160g (5¼–5¾ ounces), their normal midwinter weight in this country. At 350,000, the knot has the second largest wintering population of waders in this country.

Sanderling *Calidris alba*

Like the knot, the sanderling is almost completely confined to the coast in winter, but its population is far smaller, an average figure of 10,300 being quoted for the period 1969–75. Sometimes confused with the

Dunlin (*Calidris alpina*) in summer.

dunlin, it can be distinguished by its light grey colour, marked black shoulder feathers and restless, quick-moving, mechanical gait. It also has a characteristic habit of running into the edge of shallow water as small wavelets break on the shore. This disturbs the sand and exposes the crustacean *Corophium* upon which it feeds.

The sanderling migrates to the Arctic in late spring when the female is reported to produce two clutches of eggs in separate nests, each apparently brooded by one of the parents.

Dunlin *Calidris alpina*

This is the commonest British wader, with a winter population of 500,000. It also exhibits the fascinating flight behaviour of the knot. Grey-brown above and white below in winter, it acquires a black waistcoat and bright rusty back and wings in summer. It feeds on small shore crabs and other small crustaceans and molluscs.

Two populations are found in the British Isles: the Lapland form (*Calidris alpina alpina*), which is a winter migrant, leaving in April or May and returning in late October, and the southern form (*Caldris alpina schinzii*), which is a summer resident. This latter population is made up of between 4,000 and 8,000 pairs, most of which breed on moorland areas. However, a number of pairs breed on the larger salt marshes in the north of Britain, their nests often set within yards of those of the redshank and plover.

4 SALT MARSHES, MUDFLATS AND SHINGLE

Salt marshes

Salt marshes are tracts of land periodically immersed by the sea and colonised by flowering plants. On the extensive marshes of the Dee estuary and Morecambe Bay in Lancashire the green sward dissected by creeks seems to extend endlessly, giving way to mudflats only on the horizon. Adjacent to the sward the mud is dotted with succulents such as marsh samphire and seablite. Farther out these are replaced by green seaweeds and worms, crustaceans and molluscs that are capable of coping with the shifting mud and varying salinity of estuaries.

Salt marshes have been described as dull places characterised by the smell of decay, with a mass of plants coloured grey by coatings of silt. But those who know the marshes will remember the white flowers of scurvy grass in spring, the undulating pink meadows of thrift in late May and the purple islands of sea lavender in July contrasting with the aromatic silver spikes of sea wormwood. In addition, there is the sense of remoteness and the peace of these wild places. They are not without sound however. Skylarks and meadow pipits are common, and the patient observer may well be rewarded by the sight of a pair of shelducks leading their family down a creek to the sea. In winter oystercatchers and redshanks pipe their way down the estuary, and the mudflats are thronged with curlews, plovers and a host of other waders. In February the marshes or 'merse' of the Solway estuary are always worth a visit to see the thousands of black-and-white barnacle geese or the greylags and pinkfeet cropping the grasses and clover of the upper marsh.

Formation

The basic requirement for the formation of a salt marsh is a flattish shore with a gentle

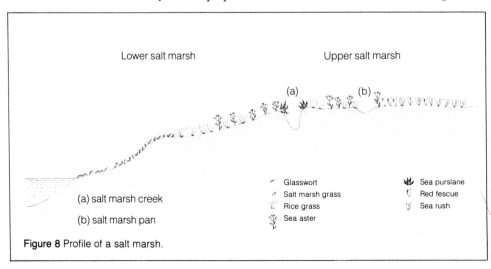

Lower salt marsh   Upper salt marsh

(a) salt marsh creek

(b) salt marsh pan

⌐	Glasswort	⚘	Sea purslane
⚘	Salt marsh grass	ⱱ	Red fescue
ⱳ	Rice grass	ⱴ	Sea rush
⚘	Sea aster		

Figure 8 Profile of a salt marsh.

slope, so that as the sea slops in the waves cause little disturbance and provide a supply of mobile mud and sand. Salt marshes are of two types. First there are those located behind shingle bars or sand spits, such as the Norfolk marshes at Blakeney Point and Scolt Head Island, or the marshes of the Dyfi (Dovey) estuary and those in the lee of Walney Island in Cumbria. Then there are the sheltered estuaries and quiet embayments typified by the marshes of Southampton Water, Morecambe Bay and the Solway estuary.

Development

Silt, mud and sand carried in suspension are responsible for the build-up of salt marshes. It is exciting to watch the movement of the tide as it flows into a sheltered area of muddy sand. The speed is sufficient to keep the sediment suspended and yet hardly a ripple is seen.

At the slackwater of high tide the sediment is dropped and is left behind as the tide ebbs. The marsh below the flowering plant vegetation is usually strewn with a variety of green seaweeds such as sea lettuce, gutweed (*Enteromorpha*), *Vaucheria*, *Ulothrix* and *Rhizoclonium*. These seaweeds bind the mud so that small hummocks develop, which themselves determine the course of shallow channels created by erosion of the unconsolidated silt on the ebb tide. The colonisation of these hummocks by pioneer species of flowering plants, such as marsh samphire, rice grass or salt marsh grass, stabilises them and leads to more efficient trapping of sediment, while the shallow channels are further deepened by tidal scour. Thus the seaward edge of the marsh is extended and a system of creeks draining it is created.

In older parts of the marsh, where a 'closed' continuous vegetational cover is established, plants are able to grow across creeks, causing blockages and sometimes creating a linear series of pools or salt marsh pans. These are often very salty and support few plants. The further development of the marsh depends upon the accumulation of sediment. Initially the build-up is fairly rapid, but as the level of the marsh increases it is less frequently covered by the tide and so sediment is deposited less often.

Tides and water supply

Salt marshes usually have a general slope towards the sea and extend between HWNTL and HWSTL. The lower parts of the marsh are, therefore, inundated more frequently than the upper ones. Working at Scolt Head in Norfolk, V.J. Chapman found that in the period from 31 July to 9 October the lower part of the marsh colonised by seaweeds was submerged for 282 out of a possible 732 hours, while the top of the marsh was submerged for about three hours per month only. The upper or emergent marsh (down to MHWL) is covered by sea water only at the highest spring tides, when it is available for seed germination and seed dispersal. The lower or submergent marsh (up to MHWL) receives water throughout most of the year and is less likely to suffer drought conditions in the growing season.

An annual, such as marsh samphire or glasswort, which colonises the mud at the lower end requires the marsh to be exposed for a minimum period of three days for the germination and establishment of seedlings, otherwise they get washed out.

Water supply is complicated by the water table level of the marsh and by water movement along the creeks. The rate of movement of underground water is in turn affected by the soil structure of the marsh – that is, by the proportion of sand to silt.

Salinity

The salinity of the ground water in a marsh is affected by the frequency of tidal flooding. Furthermore, it is concentrated by drought and diluted by heavy rainfall. Thus the osmotic pressure of the soil solution varies greatly and plants growing in it need to cope

not only with solutions much stronger than sea water but with a whole range of concentrations, some of which are weaker. As a result, certain marsh plants – known as halophytes, from the Greek *hals* (salt) and *phuton* (plant) – have evolved a number of physiological and structural adaptations to cope with these problems.

Vegetation zones

The various factors noted above, together with the competition for space between the individual species, account for the distribution of vegetation of the marsh. This takes the form of a series of vegetational zones, usually determined by height above sea level and therefore the frequency of submergence and exposure. Each zone is characterised by one or

Left Marsh samphire (*Salicornia* spp) – adult plant in mid-August growing on shingle and mud.

Below Perennial sea spurrey (*Spergularia media*) in May.

more dominant plant species. As sediment accumulates, one vegetational zone or group of plants is replaced by another in a sequence of successions or changes. A zone dominated by sea rush (*Juncus maritima*) represents the final stage. Such a sequential change is known as seral succession and when it involves salt marsh plants it is known as halosere. The pattern of succession on the more muddy east coast marshes differs in detail from that of the more sandy south and west coast situations, although the overall principle is the same. The pattern shown in the diagram is typical of west coast salt marshes. Parts of the Lancashire salt marshes in the Morecambe Bay area around Pilling, Cockerham and Silverdale are given particular mention as these are good examples of grazed marshes. The Site of Special Scientific Interest at Barnaby Sands and the salt marsh at Skipool Creek in the Wyre estuary are marshes not grazed by stock.

The relationships of the major salt marsh zones on the west coast

Zone 1 The initial stabilisation of the mud by green algae has already been discussed. In some parts of the British Isles the seaweed community is replaced by eel grasses, the only flowering salt water plants. They suffered badly from disease in the 1930s, but are reported to be recovering in some areas now.

Zone 2 The succession labelled 1(a) in the centre of the diagram is characteristic of west coast salt marshes. On the Morecambe Bay marshes at Pilling and Silverdale either glasswort (*Salicornia* spp) or glasswort and common salt marsh grass (*Puccinellia maritima* – also called sea manna grass) succeeds the seaweeds. The vegetational cover is patchy, the plants are often uprooted and tidal submergence is frequent.

Zone 3 With a slight increase in the height of the marsh, salt marsh grass soon dominates. Saltwort (*Glaux maritima*) and occasional plants of sea aster (*Aster tripolium*) can also be found. Except at the marsh at Barnaby Sands, neither sea lavender nor sea purslane is evident.

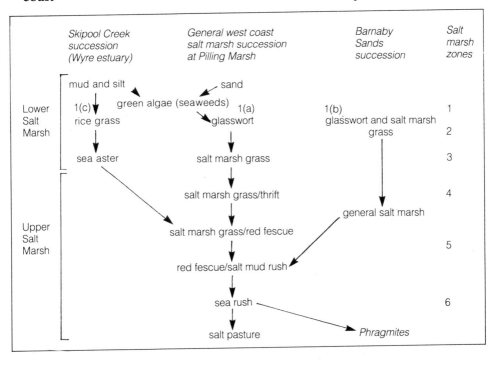

Zone 4 The pink haze of thrift (*Armeria maritima*) over large areas of the marsh in May shows that it shares much of the higher marsh with salt marsh grass. In the creeks salt mud rush (*Juncus Gerardii*), scurvy grass (*Cochleria officinalis*) and sea spurrey (*Spergularia maritima*) are common. Most of these plants are relatively small specimens, almost certainly because of intensive sheep grazing. Grazing also causes large areas of dense fescue turf to develop. This is widely sold as 'sea washed turf' and is much prized by horticulturists.

Zones 4 and 5 The marsh now grades into a vegetation dominated by salt marsh grass and red fescue (*Festuca rubra*) with a fair amount of salt mud rush (*Juncus Gerardii*) in places, finally grading into a zone dominated by sea rush (*Juncus maritima*). However, these zones do not occur as a series of clearly defined bands. Rather, they form a mosaic of vegetational types, each group of plants dominating where local variations in the height of the marsh favour their development. A variety of subordinate plants are associated with the red fescue zone, including sea plantain (*Plantago maritima*), buckshorn plantain (*Plantago coronopus*), sea arrow grass (*Triglochin maritima*) and sea sedge (*Carex maritima*).

Zone 6 The sea rush zone represents the ultimate stage in the development of the salt marsh proper. Among the rushes sea aster (*Aster tripolium*), scurvy grass, sea sedge and marsh bedstraw (*Galium palustre*) can be found. The whole of the upper marsh area grades into salt pasture, which is a mixture of salt marsh and meadow species. A reclamation project involving the building of a great earth bank to exclude the sea in the Pilling area during the late 1970s has completely ruined the view out to sea, and the marsh vegetation has also changed. However, the above description still holds good for much of the Morecambe Bay marsh system.

Sea arrow grass (*Triglochin maritima*).

At Barnaby Sands – the succession labelled 1(b) to the right of the diagram – the lushness, vigour and relatively larger size of the plants encountered at Pilling is striking. Rice grass, glasswort and salt marsh grass occur early in the succession and thrift is common but does not dominate, as it does at Pilling. Instead, there appears to be a general mixture of salt marsh plants in the upper marsh, usually with no species clearly dominating. They include sea lavender (*Limonium* spp), sea arrow grass, sea aster, sea plantain, saltwort (*Glaux maritima*), sea purslane, scurvy grass, seablite (*Suaeda maritima*) and one or two species of orache (*Atriplex* spp). Certain areas are colonised exclusively by the various species of sea lavender or by sea wormwood. Sea purslane (*Halimione portulacoides*) forms beautiful silvery-grey shoulders on the creek banks where the sharp drainage and its shrubby habit allow it to dominate.

An alternative primary coloniser of salt marshes, particularly where an abundance of mud is available, is rice grass (*Spartina* × *townsendii*). This plant is a hybrid between *S. maritima* (European cord grass) and *S. alterniflora* (American cord grass) and was first recognised in Southampton Water in 1870. Like most hybrids it is more vigorous than either parent. In the 1950s it was reported as having spread into Morecambe Bay. Whether this was by natural means or whether it was spread artificially by those wishing to reclaim land is not known, but by then it had become well established in the Ribble and Wyre estuaries and around Pilling.

Its ability to accumulate mud on the previously more sandy foreshore at Lytham was such that the local civic society established a research grant in 1967 at Lancaster University to see how it could be removed. At Skipool Creek in the Wyre estuary succession 1(c) is initiated by a broad band of almost pure rice grass which gives way to a narrow band of sea purslane extending along the creeks. Between this narrow band and the retaining wall running parallel to the river there is an area dominated by red fescue, with many of the species noted for the general salt marsh zone at Barnaby Sands.

How different Skipool Creek would look now to the sea captains of the slave trade who once used it as a port. These 'blackbirders' took Lancashire's cotton goods to West Africa, traded them for slaves and sold the slaves for raw cotton, which they brought back to Skipool Creek. Some of these captains retired and bought small farms in the Pilling area, as evidenced by the names Louisiana Farm and Kentucky Farm clearly noted on the six inch Ordnance Survey map.

If you stand by an estuarine salt marsh when a high spring tide is running late in September, in no time at all, it seems, the narrow river channel spreads to become a lake, covering the mudflats. Then the walls of the creeks fill and spill over, yet still the water rises. You can see the water buoying up the plants, the fruits and seeds being gently lifted off their submerging branches. Soon all that can be seen is a great sheet of water from bank to bank peppered with fruits and seeds, which the tidal currents disperse.

Succession

It was once believed that salt marsh developed into reed swamp, which was subsequently colonised by willow, alder and various herbs to form carr which later developed into woodland. Carr is a vegetation composed of small trees that can tolerate high water tables, such as alder, willow and birch, with herbs typical of marsh or swamp growing among the trees and with ferns, mosses and lichens growing on the lower branches in response to the high humidity.

But the juxtaposition of reed swamp, fen, carr and woodland is not in itself evidence that one vegetational type gives rise to another. The theory that salt marsh develops into reed swamp and that carr is subsequently formed is supported by examination of fossilised coastal sediments, together with pollen analysis. However, that carr develops into woodland is highly questionable. Acidification and the formation of coastal mire and bog dominated by *Sphagnum* is much more likely.

Animal life

Most studies of the animal life of salt marshes focus on the organisms inhabiting mudflats rather than the salt marsh vegetation. However, the relationship between the animal life of the salt marshes and salt meadows is very interesting. Both terrestrial and aquatic invertebrate species are found right across the marsh, from the rice grass at the seaward edge and on the creek sides to the salt pasture of the high marsh.

A visit to an estuary on a high spring tide is very exciting. From suitable vantage points all manner of animals, including small mammals,

Sea lavender (*Limonium* spp).

Sea purslane (*Halimione portulacoides*). The silvery leaves owe their colour to special hairs which cover their surfaces to reduce water loss.

can be seen emerging from the marsh vegetation. Some fly, others climb up the vegetation, many swim or, as the tide rises, walk on the water surface. Certain mites are known to survive periods of submergence of up to twelve weeks. Many of these small animals are typical marsh species, however, and do not have any special affinity with brackish or saline conditions.

A simple food chain based on a study of a recently established rice grass marsh in Dorset looks like this:

Rice grass ➤ Herbivorous bug ➤ Omnivorous
grasshopper
↓
Marsh
damsel bug

A more extensive study of the relationship of salt meadow flora and fauna carried out by K. Paviour-Smith in New Zealand suggests that the detritus produced from plant decay makes an important contribution to the richness of the salt marsh community. Other more recent studies support this view. The increase in the amount and quality of protein made available by microbial conversion also appears to be of great significance to the whole ecosystem.

Birds

Many migrant wildfowl species use the marshes as temporary winter residences – both as roosting sites and as valuable feeding stations.

Ducks

Mallard (*Anas platyrhynchos*) and teal (*Anas crecca*) feed on orache seeds and on those of clover and creeping buttercup higher up the marsh on the salt pasture. Pintail (*Anas acuta*) take underwater plant material and various plant seeds on coastal marshes. Wigeon (*Anas penelope*) may also do so, though they prefer to graze eel grass and the alga called gutweed (*Enteromorpha*), so named because it resembles unravelled intestines.

Above Teal (*Anas crecca*), one of the smallest British ducks, can often be observed feeding on salt marshes.

Below Mud trapping rice grass.

Brent goose *Branta bernicla*

The Brent goose takes the same food as the ducks. About 140,000 migrate from the high Arctic to the south-east coast of Britain each year. They start by feeding on eel grass beds and green algae, but once this resource is exhausted they move on to glasswort, salt marsh grass and the red fescue (*Festuca rubra*) of the fringing salt marsh.

Greylag goose *Anser anser*

Canada goose *Branta canadensis*

Higher up on the marshes the relatively large-billed geese such as Canadas and greylags are found not only feeding on the leaves of rice grass, bulrushes and reedmace but also digging for roots and the fat underground stems or rhizomes of plants rich in starch.

Pinkfoot goose *Anser brachyrhynchus*

Widespread reclamation of marshes has caused greylag and pinkfoot geese to become more adapted to farmland, and valuable winter feed is obtained from cornfield stubble and reject tubers lying in the potato fields. The popularity of this food is reflected in the record of 32,680 pinkfeet in a field near the Martin Mere Reserve in Lancashire in December 1982. However, these birds often roost on the marshes and 25,000 pinkfeet were recorded on the Solway estuary at Caerlaverock in January 1984.

Barnacle goose *Branta leucopsis*

In 1963 it was established that the whole barnacle goose population of the Svalbard archipelago overwinters in the Solway Firth. The population has risen from 300 birds in the 1940s to 9,050 recorded in 1982. Apart from man, the barnacle goose has few predators in this country, although recently a peregrine (not usually regarded as a carrion feeder) was observed feeding on a barnacle carcass, the inference being that the goose had been killed by the falcon.

Barnacles arrive in late September and, after first gleaning the cornfields, move on to the upper shore salt marshes or merse, taking the leaves and starch-rich stolons (creeping stems) of white clover and feeding on meadow grasses at high tide. The goose has a vigorous feeding mechanism (200 pecks a minute) and the long migration (2,000 miles) precludes the development of a sophisticated digestive system, so that much of its faecal material consists of only partially digested food, with the result that the bird seeds its own feeding ground. The rich winter feeding builds up fat reserves – important to breeding females, since this may determine the number of eggs laid in the Arctic nesting grounds.

Barnacle geese fly north in March. The first stage of the journey – 1,000 miles to Norwegian offshore islands – is completed in only twenty-four hours. Here young grass shoots provide food for further fattening. The remaining 1,000 miles is completed in five weeks. Spitsbergen, like the other islands of the Svalbard archipelago, is a series of isolated islands where the goose finds little competition for food. The frozen sub-soil impedes drainage, creating pools and lakes which 'moat' nesting sites and provide protection from the only ground predator, the Arctic fox. Bird predators include glaucous gulls, ravens and larger skuas. The Arctic climate is the principal disadvantage, since a maximum July temperature of 10°C means that the Arctic vegetation is slow growing. However, it is sufficient to fulfil the food requirements of the barnacles. The breeding season is also short. It starts after the spring thaw, which begins in June, and must be completed before the winter snows, which start in August.

Mudflats

In broad, flattish estuaries and sheltered bays salt marshes give way at their seaward edge to extensive areas of mudflats. These areas are characterised by the absence of flowering plants. Microscopic algae, including bottom-living diatoms, are common in such areas and

Shelduck (*Tadorna tadorna*) – a common duck of mudflats and salt marshes.

contribute significantly to the basic food resources. The fine organic mud provides rich raw material for bacteria to feed on. They convert this into their own body materials, which represents an upgrading in the type of proteins available for larger animals. The fine silt in turn provides a large surface area for both the bacteria and the microscopic algae to grow on – so that the mudflats, although at first glance they appear to lack any significant plant food resource, represent a reasonably productive environment. A third food source is the phytoplankton suspended in the sea water when it covers the mudflats.

Many of the animals already encountered on mud-enriched sandy shores are also found here, including ragworms, lugworms, cockles, Baltic tellins, shrimps, shore crabs and other smaller crustaceans. Like the sand dwellers, the mudflat animals have an interesting variety of feeding strategies.

Detritus feeders

At least one estuarine animal, the small snail *Hydrobia ulvae* feeds on micro-organisms in the organic mud, digesting them out of the detritus. This is nutritionally advantageous, as the micro-organisms represent a better quality of food than the plant material which they decompose. It may be that other detritus-feeding animals do the same. Rarely more than 4·5mm (1/5 inch) in height, this small snail can easily be overlooked, yet on the Clyde estuary it has been recorded in densities of up to 42,000 animals per square metre and it is an important food item for a number of estuarine birds, especially the shelduck.

Two other detritus-feeding molluscs of the

Barnacle geese (*Branta leucopsis*) feeding.

mudflats are the Baltic tellin and the peppery furrow shell. The feeding methods of the tellins is described in Chapter 3.

Peppery furrow shell

Scrobicularia plana da Costa

This animal has an oval, flattened shell up to 6.25cm (2½ inches) long, light in colour and scored with concentric lines on the outer surface. Its siphons are phenomenally long, extending to 15 or 20cm (6–8 inches). Their activities leave a series of linear grooves in the mud radiating from a central hole where the animal is buried. It may be up to 15cm (6 inches) beneath the surface, safe from predators. It feeds on detritus deposited on the mud by using its siphon like a vacuum cleaner.

Corophium spp

This detritus-feeding crustacean, which lacks a common name, is an important member of

the estuarine food web (another is the water shrimp *Gammarus* described in Chapter 3). *Corophium* is up to 8mm (⅓ inch) in length and, like *Hydrobia*, it may be present in vast numbers – indeed, as many as 28,000 per square metre have been found in parts of the Ythan estuary, just north of Aberdeen. These are probably the commonest sand and mud-dwelling animals in non-polluted estuaries.

Corophium has a pair of well-developed antennae, almost half its body length, which it uses to move over the mud in a series of looping movements. They are also used for burrowing. Once its U-shaped burrow has been excavated, the burrow walls are held in position by a sticky substance produced by the animal.

Different species are confined to particular substrates. Thus, *C. volutator* is found on fine sand or mud, while *C. arenarium* selects coarser clean sand. When covered in water the animal swims towards the light, but it burrows away from the light when it is exposed to air. This permits the tiny

Specimen shells of mudflat bivalve molluscs: clam (*Mya arenaria*), peppery furrow shell (*Scrobicularia plana da Costa*) and common mussel (*Mytilus edulis*).

crustacean to swim at high tide and to hide away from predators when the mudflats are exposed.

Filter feeders

Three bivalve molluscs typical of mudflats use this feeding strategy. Filter feeders remove the food material suspended in sea water, such as phytoplankton and zooplankton. Mussels have already been described in Chapter 2 and cockles in Chapter 3. The gaper, or clam, is typical of mud-rich sand or stiff mud, according to the species.

Clams *Mya arenaria*

This is the animal favoured by the Americans for their clam-bakes. When young it has a large foot and moves around actively. As it matures, it embeds itself deep in stiff mud and becomes more passive. Its siphons are joined together along their length and are fringed with tentacles at their free end. They are seen as a double-mouthed opening at the surface of the mud. The siphons may be up to 30cm (12 inches) in length. The clam is the largest British bivalve and shells of good specimens

may measure 15cm by 8cm (6 by 3 inches). A dead colony around which the mud has been eroded is exposed at low tide on the Duddon estuary at Askam, Cumbria, where the animals are still fixed *in situ* as they appeared in life. Smaller specimens of most of these deposit and filter-feeding animals are taken by ragworms and shore crabs. They are also eaten by the principal predators of mudflat communities – fish and birds.

Fish as mudflat predators

Goby *Gobius minutus*

The common goby already described as an inhabitant of rocky shores can also be found in estuaries, especially in autumn. Its relative the black goby (*G. niger*) seems to particularly favour estuarine habitats. Both these fish feed on lugworms and ragworms, and take a variety of crustaceans too. In winter when the weather is severe they retreat into deeper, more saline and warmer waters.

Flounder *Platychthes flesus*

The flounder is another estuarine fish which can penetrate quite a way up rivers. This is probably the reason why it takes gnat larvae as food.

At about two months old the symmetrical pelagic larval fish start to metamorphose into flatfish. The left eye usually migrates to the right-hand side of the head and the fish begins to swim right-hand side uppermost. This upper surface develops a dark pigmentation. The larval fish are now about 12–14mm ($^{1}/_{2}$ inch) long and abandon their pelagic existence, migrate to shallow coastal waters and start to live on the sea bottom.

The habit of swimming right-hand side up is a characteristic shared with its relative the plaice (*Pleuronectes platessa*). However, the flounder can be identified by the roughness of its skin, particularly along the lateral line and the base of the dorsal fin. Hybrids between the two occur and possess smoother skin than the flounder and less prominent red spots than the plaice. Younger flounders feed mainly on small crustaceans, although older fish take typical mudflat prey items such as lugworms, ragworms, tellins and even gobies. As the flounder achieves population peaks on mudflats in summer rather than autumn, when gobies are abundant, the predation pressure on the mudflat is spread a little. Like gobies, flounders move into deeper water in winter, leaving the food resource to that other group of mudflat predators – the waders.

Birds feeding on mudflats

Waders

A whole range of waders overwinter on the mudflats of estuaries, although the populations of the different species appear to peak at different times for relatively short periods. Again this spreads the predation pressure. Wader species such as the redshank, dunlin, knot, curlew, golden plover, lapwing, oystercatcher and turnstone appear regularly and in significant numbers. Of the waders, the turnstone has been considered in Chapter 2 and the oystercatcher is discussed under mussel beds below and again in Chapter 6. Dunlin and knot are discussed in Chapter 3.

Redshank *Tringa totanus*

Slightly smaller than the oystercatcher, this beautiful wader with an evocative call is found in substantial numbers on estuarine flats in winter, particularly in the north. Its medium-length reddish beak and red legs contrast with its grey-brown body, allowing ready identification.

Detailed studies of the feeding habits of the redshank were made in the Ythan estuary near Aberdeen by J.D. Goss-Custard (*see* bibliography). At temperatures above 6°C *Corophium* was found to be the most important food item of the redshank, and indeed by March it was found that 16 per cent of the October population of *Corophium* had

been removed. However, this level of predation was not thought to have been sufficient to impair the feeding efficiency of the bird.

In March many redshanks move to upland areas to breed, and for many years I have been rewarded by the sound of their mournful piping when visiting Cronkley Fell in Upper Teesdale in summer. Some, however, remain to breed on salt marshes and moist meadows along river valleys.

Ringed plover *Charadrius hiaticula*

Smaller than the redshank this diminutive bird can be recognised by its black collar and black-and-white head, which contrast with its brown body and yellow legs. It is fairly common on mudflats and sandy coasts, particularly in northern England and Scotland, although it is said to be scarce in the southwest. It feeds on a variety of invertebrates on or near the surface of the mud and nests in sand or gravel, forming a number of scrapes into one of which it lays three or four black-spotted eggs with an olive-brown ground colour. Incubation lasts for twenty-four days and a similar period is taken for fledging.

Curlew *Numenius arquata*

This is perhaps the most exciting and largest of all waders visiting the coast in winter. Its bubbling call, which delights us on a summer moorland where it breeds, is always a welcome sound echoing across the misty November mudflats. Few invertebrates can escape the deep searching of its long, curved beak. In common with godwits and oystercatchers, it takes both lugworms and ragworms and cockles and mussels.

Shelduck *Tadorna tadorna*

The wildfowl most commonly associated with mudflats is one of the largest British ducks, the shelduck. Its bottle-green head contrasts with its scarlet bill, and the overall black-and-white appearance is relieved by a

Above Ringed plover (*Charadrius hiaticula*) on nest.

Right Curlew (*Numenius arquata*) – common on salt marshes in winter.

bright orange-brown band round the forepart of the body. Despite the bird's large size, 40 per cent of its food consists of the tiny snail *Hydrobia*. It feeds by inserting its bill just below the mud and making scything movements with its head, detecting the molluscs with its sensitive bill tip and tongue. The sight of hundreds of these birds on the mud-flats illuminated by the sun on an autumn morning is a magnificent spectacle.

Mussel beds

Where stable shingle beds are associated with the mud they provide a suitable base for the attachment of mussels. Most of the other invertebrates typical of mudflat communities are also present and the edible crab, the periwinkle, gammarids and *Corophium* are significant elements in the diet of mussel bed predators.

Eider *Somateria mollisima*

Another large British duck, the eider, is an important predator of mussels. The brown female is well camouflaged at nesting time and contrasts beautifully with the black-and-white

Above Oystercatcher (*Haematopus ostralegus*).

Below Seablite (*Sueada maritima*).

male, which has a green patch at the back of is head in the breeding season.

Eiders feed either by dabbling in the shallow water of ebbing tides or diving deep in sub-littoral waters on the flood. They take mussels averaging 18mm (¾ inch) in length but can cope with specimens twice that size, swallowing them whole and crushing them in their powerful gizzards. The down of the eider, which the bird uses in nest building, is very soft and warm and is collected for quilts, duvets and pillows.

Oystercatcher *Haematopus ostralegus*

This large, handsome, black-and-white wader feeds on mussels exposed at low tide, using its long, strong red bill to hammer on the shells

to split them. The average length of mussels taken by oystercatchers is 33mm (1¼ inches), but specimens up to 70mm (2¾ inches) are also consumed.

Herring gull *Larus argentatus*

Herring gulls also feed on mussels, swallowing very small specimens – up to 10mm (²⁄₅ inch) – whole and breaking open larger

Eider duck (*Somateria mollissima*) mimicking a lump of driftwood while incubating her eggs.

ones by dropping them from a great height onto stones or hard sand.

The diagram illustrates the feeding relationships (food web) of the animals of the mudflats:

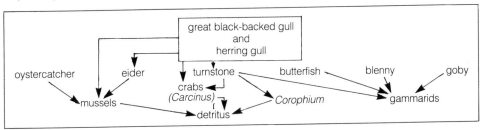

Shingle spits and banks

Probably the best known shingle bank in Britain is Chesil Beach, which stretches nine miles from the Isle of Portland to the swannery at Abbotsbury in Dorset. Others are Dungeness, a great wild area off the south coast of Kent, and Spurn Point, which curves into the Humber estuary and protects the richly vegetated salt marshes which have developed on its lee side.

Because shingle is unstable it is unsuitable for colonisation by plants. Also, its relatively coarse nature precludes the upward capillary movement of moisture from the water table below. Thus aridity is added to instability – and the dearth of flowering plants suggests an absence of humus too.

Formation of shingle banks

Shingle is thrown up into great banks by the sea and is scoured into a series of terraces. As the tidal pattern moves from springs to neaps, each terrace marks the position of the previous high tide. At this time organic matter is deposited among the shingle and, as successively higher tides occur, the material is either buried or washed into the shingle by sea or rain. During storms shingle is piled up and, given an adequate supply of raw material, new high ridges are created which stand well above the reach of all but the highest spring tides. Thus for a time a more stable regime is produced, particularly on the lee slopes of the bank. This apparently inhospitable environment is not, therefore, so unfriendly to living organisms as you might think; and in the lee of the bank encrusting lichens develop on undisturbed stones, while on the terraces individual plants or small communities of vegetation can occur.

Shingle banks warm up quickly in the sun and this probably accounts for the breakdown of organic material into humus, which can be seen if you remove a few stones to reveal the fine coating of debris below. These buried stones are usually moist or wet near the top of a high bank, even though they are well above the water table – probably as a result of condensation caused by the action of the stones.

Thus moisture, stability and humus that will retain mineral salts from sea spray and air may all be available at least locally on shingle banks, accounting for the discontinuous or open nature of the vegetation. Poor in species, shingle nevertheless carries a range of plants.

Shrubby seablite *Suaeda fruticosa*

This plant is found locally on Chesil Beach and on the Norfolk coast. Under stable conditions it grows 1 to 1·5m (3–5 feet) tall, but in more mobile shingle it is pushed over and partially buried. New lateral shoots arise from the buried stems and bunches of roots develop under each shoot, forming a system of branching, rooted vertical shoots which bind and stabilise the shingle. Sea campion (*see* Chapter 1) also favours this habitat.

Sea sandwort *Honkenya peploides*

Sea sandwort seems able to survive being buried by shingle. Its low rosette forms also help it withstand exposure to sea spray and strong winds. Extensive underground stems bind the covering shingle and produce new surface rosettes of plants in response to burial.

Yellow horned poppy
Glaucium flavum

This characteristic plant of the shingle produces vertical stems to carry its lovely yellow flowers in summer. Its grey-green hairy leaves protect it from damage by sea spray, though it seldom survives for more than a year in unstable shingle. It reproduces easily from seed, the long seed pods being responsible for its name. Unlike the previous two species, it possesses a long taproot and does not bind mobile shingle well.

Sea beet *Beta vulgaris*

Sea beet grows in shingle near the high water mark. It possesses dark green leathery leaves which are often shiny and are arranged in a basal rosette. This plant is the ancestor of sugar beet, spinach beet and beetroot.

Sea kale *Crambe maritima*

A rather substantial fleshy plant, sea kale has a huge rosette of broad blue-green leaves, the whole around 1m (39 inches) across and looking like a large cabbage, to which it is related. From this rosette stems of similar length bear heads of large white flowers from June onwards which are succeeded by egg-shaped seed pods.

Typically a plant of the strand line and shingle bank, it is more common in the south-east of the country, although it grows near

Yellow horned poppy (*Glaucium flavum*).

the North Walney reserve in Cumbria and used to be plentiful on the cliffs of south Devon. It was from here that it was introduced as a vegetable to Covent Garden in 1795 and its young shoots were eaten like asparagus. Since then it has become rare in its Devon location.

Annual glasswort (marsh samphire) *Salicornia europaea*

Most definitely a primary coloniser of salt marshes and also a shingle plant, the glasswort is a succulent with erect bright green waxy stems up to 24cm (10 inches) in height. The leaves are reduced to scales and food manufacture is taken over by the stem tissues. The inconspicuous flowers are sunk into the stem in groups of three on the tapering stem spikes. As its name implies, it was once used in the manufacture of glass and can be eaten as an unusual pickle with cold beef.

Other maritime plants found in this habitat include the oraches and grasses more commonly associated with dunes, including species of sea couch.

Plants commonly found in inland situations may also be encountered on shingle banks. Yellow stonecrop (*Sedum acre*), low growing and succulent, is ideally adapted to survive on shingle and delights us with its bright yellow flowers in summer. Silverweed, goosegrass, sowthistle and groundsel can be found in places where the vegetation is more continuous, and birdsfoot trefoil and viper's bugloss sometimes lend a delightful touch of colour to the scene.

In undisturbed shingle well away from the direct influence of the sea prostrate forms of shrubs such as broom and woody nightshade are common and provide good nesting sites for birds such as linnets (*Carduelis cannabina*) and stonechats (*Saxicola torquata*). The ringed plover (*Charadrius hiaticula*) also finds shingle beaches to its liking, as its alternative name of 'stone runner' suggests.

Above Sea kale (*Crambe maritima*).

Below Biting stonecrop (*Sedum acre*) on shingle.

5 SAND DUNES

Sand dune systems occupy extensive areas along the coasts of the British Isles. In the West Country they are often known as 'burrows', as at Braunton Burrows in Devon, for example. The word 'burrow' derives from the Old English *beorgan* (to shelter or defend) and anyone who has attempted to climb the unstable, mobile dunes will realise that they would have been difficult ramparts for an invading tribe to storm. In Scotland, dunes are referred to as 'links', derived from the Old English *hlinc*, a bank, ridge or slope. The word 'meol' or 'meal' is associated with dunes in Lancashire, from the Old English *mealm* or *meln*, meaning soft, friable earth –

perhaps a reference to the way crusted sand breaks in the fingers. On the east coast, the term 'dene', from the Old English word for a valley or den, is used. This wide variety of Old English words for dune systems is not only evidence of the existence of local dialects but also implies that only limited contact occurred between different regions of the country at that time.

Location

Sand dunes on the west coast are often extensive, like the ones at Newborough Warren, Anglesey. Over the past 300 years a belt of dunes over a mile long has built up between

Foreshore and early stages of sand dune formation, Newborough Warren, Anglesey.

Sea rocket (*Cakile maritima*).

Formby and the Ribble estuary in Lancashire; and extensive dune systems exist in Cumbria, for example to the north of Walney Island near Barrow-in-furness, at Askam on the Duddon estuary and at Ravenglass, to the south of St Bees Head.

East coast dune systems, such as those just south of Seahouses in Northumbria, tend to be smaller. However, the strip of coast between the Moray Firth and Aberdeen possesses dune systems comparable with those of the west coast.

Formation

The prime requisite for the formation of sand dunes is the availability of copious quantities of blown sand. This is found on coasts where there is a significant tidal range and a gently sloping sandy shore. Such sloping shores are by no means flat, but are sculpted into sand banks known as 'fulls' separated by channels called 'lows'. The sand on the fulls is soft and porous and dries out quickly, in contrast with the hard sand of the lows, which remains wet.

This dry sand, together with any debris resting on it or lightly buried in it, is blown up to the strand line. On the west coast, south-westerly winds carry the sand up the shore and any obstructions, such as dead seaweed, shells or discarded human materials, locally reduce the wind speed, causing some of the sand grains to be deposited. Thus, tiny mounds of sand accumulate.

The strand line

If sand is deposited above HWSTL, the mounds are unlikely to be disturbed, so that the tidal litter traps varying quantities of viable seed. Tidal litter also reduces extreme daily temperature fluctuations, providing a more equable environment in which the seeds can germinate and develop.

The plants that commonly grow in this situation are spiny saltwort (*Salsola kali*) and sea rocket (*Cakile maritima*). These are well adapted to the strand line situation and can cope with periodic immersion by very high spring tides. However, they cannot accumulate much sand around themselves and so do not contribute to the development of the dunes.

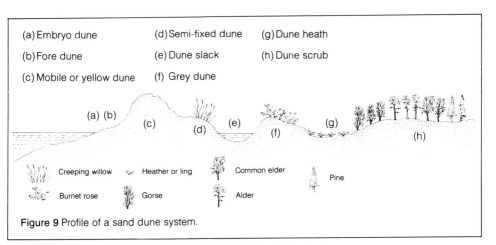

Figure 9 Profile of a sand dune system.

(a) Embryo dune (d) Semi-fixed dune (g) Dune heath
(b) Fore dune (e) Dune slack (h) Dune scrub
(c) Mobile or yellow dune (f) Grey dune

Creeping willow   Heather or ling   Common elder   Pine
Burnet rose   Gorse   Alder

Embryo dunes or foredunes

With two maritime grass species the story is somewhat different. Sea couch (*Agropyron junceforme*) and sea lime grass (*Elymus arenaria*) both tolerate inundation by the sea; and once they have germinated, the first leaves locally reduce the speed of the sand-bearing wind and cause sand to be deposited around the plants. Roots and rhizomes (underground stems) develop, the latter giving rise to further clumps of leaves. This growth system traps and binds the sand; and over a period of three to six years the development of an embryo dune between one and two metres (3–6 feet) high is quite usual. Sea couch and lime grass seem unable to continue the dune-building process beyond that height, but whether this is due to an insufficient supply of water, organic matter or nutrients, or whether at this stage they are overwhelmed by sand or shaded out by invading marram grass is uncertain. However, it is marram grass that now takes over the dune-building process.

Mobile or yellow dunes

These are the high dunes immediately on the landward side of embryo dunes. Like the fore-dunes, they are fed by and grow from sand blown onshore. Their great height is due to the tremendous growth rate of marram grass (*Ammophila arenaria*), which responds to being covered with sand by growing vertically and horizontally, binding the sand, while obtaining its water supply from its roots and rhizomes far below. In dry conditions the margins of marram leaves roll inwards to reduce water loss from the stomata on the inside surface.

The tussocks of marram are separated by large areas of bare sand and the dunes may gradually change shape under wind pressure. Occasionally great volumes of sand are excavated by the wind, creating a 'blow out'. When this happens, the complex interwoven scaffolding of the marram rhizomes is revealed.

Among the marram on the crests and lee-ward faces of these dunes perennial plants either with long taproots, such as common ragwort (*Senecio jacobaea*), or with extensive rhizomes, like creeping thistle (*Cirsium arvense*), are found. The rosette arrangement and the more divided structure of the leaves of these plants are both adaptations designed to reduce water loss. A dune dandelion (*Taraxacum laevigatum*) occurs but is smaller than its cousin and has reddish-brown seeds, in contrast to the grey-brown ones of the larger inland forms. An interesting annual plant is groundsel (*Senecio vulgaris*), which has fleshy leaves and a well-developed taproot. A characteristic but not invariable feature of the plant is the possession of ray florets as well as disc florets, making the flowers look like

Marram grass (*Ammophila arenaria*) stabilises and aids in the development of yellow dunes.

those of miniature ragwort plants. This is a genetic variation often associated with maritime conditions.

Two plants usually found only in dune systems are sea spurge (*Euphorbia paralias*) and sea holly (*Eryngium maritimum*). Sea spurge has fleshy, waxy leaves and a long taproot. The shoot, when picked, exudes a milky latex characteristic of this plant family, which also includes the rubber tree. The leaves of sea holly are also waxy and bear a series of spines, which reduce the leaf area and also protect the plant from grazing animals. Its edible roots used to be dug up and candied in Tudor times and were known as 'eringo' roots. The aerial parts of sea holly are popular with flower arrangers.

Both these plants, like the ones described earlier, possess xerophytic characteristics – that is, their leaves and stems are adapted to reduce water loss. This is not surprising when it is realised that they grow in soil containing less than one per cent humus – the material which retains moisture in soil. Moreover, soil temperatures in excess of 40°C may be experienced in summer, and often the only source of water is that which forms as dew. The soil of a mobile dune is rich in broken shell fragments, the high calcium content of which accounts for its alkalinity. The significance of this is discussed below.

Semi-fixed dunes

Semi-fixed dunes are intermediate in type between yellow dunes and fixed or grey dunes. They have extensive but not complete vegetational cover, and the soils are less alkaline and contain slightly more organic material than those of yellow dunes. Most of the plants already described are found here too.

Sand sedge (*Carex arenaria*) produces a series of aerial shoots arranged in a straight line along the path of its underground rhizome. Like all sedges, it has leaves arranged in three

Sea spurge (*Euphorbia paralias*).

Wild or heartsease pansy (*Viola tricolor* subspp *Curtisii*).

ranks and a stem which is triangular in section. In contrast, grasses have leaves arranged in two ranks and stems which are round in section. Scarlet pimpernel (*Anagallis arvensis*) brightens these dunes as does common centaury (*Centaurium erythraea*), while the soft, hairy heads of haresfoot clover (*Trifolium arvense*) are always a delight to encounter. In spring the heartsease pansy (*Viola tricolor*), in all its colour forms, gives a lovely purple blush to the dunes. Its relative the dune dog violet (*Viola canina*) can be distinguished from it by the yellow spur projecting from the back of the flower.

Hound's tongue *Cynoglossum officinale*

Not to be missed in June is the occasional plant of hound's tongue. These plants are about 60 to 80cm (24–31 inches) high and the lower leaves are covered with a dense felt of hair and arranged in a rosette – adaptations which reduce water loss. The flowers are a

sullen red colour and are later replaced by four flat seeds covered with tiny hooks, imparting a roughness like the texture of a hound's tongue. According to Culpepper, the leaves boiled in wine could cure abdominal pain and were employed both as a purgative and as a cure for diarrhoea. This concoction was also believed to be an antidote to a bite from a mad dog. The bruised leaves were said to heal 'green wounds' and the baked root, ground and made into a paste, was used to relieve piles.

Rest harrow *Ononis repens*

Rest harrow is a hairy, shrubby plant with grey-green leaves, about 30 to 60cm (1–2 feet) high but of semi-prostrate form. One form of the plant has spiny stems. A member of the pea family, it possesses pink-purple flowers about 10mm ($^2/_5$ inch) in diameter. The name rest harrow is thought to have been given to the plant by early agriculturists because the

Sea holly (*Eryngium maritimum*).

Hound's tongue (*Cynoglossum officinale*).

long fibrous rhizomes were so tough that they arrested the harrow.

In spring many small annual plants flower on the dunes including a tiny member of the wallflower family, spring whitlow grass (*Erophila verna*). The early forget-me-not, field speedwell and rue-leaved saxifrage are also common.

Stable or grey dunes

Stable dunes are lower in height than yellow dunes and form the most landward series of dune ridges. Organically richer, having 5 per cent humus, the soils are also less alkaline as a result of the calcium salts being washed out. The soil below the vegetation is cool and moist, and plant roots are usually concentrated in the top twelve inches. Soil stability discourages marram, which appears only in isolated tufts on stable dunes, the main grasses being red fescue and Yorkshire fog. The vegetational cover is almost continuous and the name of grey dunes is due to the presence of mosses and lichens. One of these, the dog lichen (*Peltigera canina*), forms overlapping grey sheets, which are veined on the under-surface and possess reddish-brown fruiting bodies at their tips.

The grey dunes are very rich in plant species of many families, including a number of orchids, the three common buttercups, and self-heal and thyme from the nettle family. Rest harrow is joined by birdsfoot trefoil (*Lotus corniculatus*) with its lovely clusters of yellow flowers tinged with carmine, which are perhaps responsible for its other name of 'eggs and bacon'. Two more lime-loving (calcicolous) members of the pea family, kidney vetch (*Anthyllis vulneraria*) and spring vetch (*Vicia lathyroides*), enrich the dune soil by fixing nitrogen by means of bacteria carried in nodules on their roots. Other calcicoles include the brightly coloured yellowwort, while common and sea centaury, autumn fellwort and carline thistle add pink, mauve and purple. Representatives of the dandelion family include daisies and hardheads, cat's ear, hawkbit and fleabane. Another member of this family is chicory (*Cichorium intybus*), whose stems up to 1m (3 feet) high bear flowers ranging in colour from mid-blue to purple. Chicory roots are dried and ground to make the commercial coffee substitute.

Asparagus *Asparagus officinalis*

Asparagus occurs naturally on grey dunes in some localities, though its natural distribution is obscure because it often escapes from gardens. In the wild the plant grows as a ferny bush, 1–1·5m (3–5 feet) high, with its leaves reduced to fine needles, well adapted to its dune habitat and very different from the cultivated form eaten as a vegetable. Individual plants are either male or female.

Partial parasites

Yellow rattle (*Rhinanthus minor*) grows up to 20cm (8 inches) tall. Its small yellow flowers peep out from an inflated green calyx, which turns brown and rattles on seeding. Another member of the foxglove family, eyebright (*Euphrasia officinalis*), is half as tall, with tiny white flowers marked with yellow and purple. The juice of this plant was once used as a cure for eye ailments. Both these plants are partial parasites, producing their own food above ground but tapping the roots of grasses for their supply of water and mineral salts.

Evening primrose *Oenothera biennis*

An import from North America, the evening primrose is found on a number of Lancashire and Merseyside sand dune systems. Its lovely large yellow flowers are said to open in the evening for pollination by moths. However, the flowers open at all times of the day, and it may be that the governing factor is humidity and that pollination is, in fact, effected by other groups of insects.

Spiny and sprawling thorn-bearing shrubby plants also grow on grey dunes. They include the bramble (*Rubus fruticosus*) and its relative the dewberry (*Rubus caesus*). In the northwest and on the east coast another beautiful shrub of the rose family, burnet rose (*Rosa spinossisima*), is common. In autumn it bears the characteristic reddish-black hips popular in flower arrangements.

Dune scrub

In the absence of heavy grazing, dune scrub develops on grey dunes. Elder (*Sambucus nigra*) is typical, while other small shrubs such as gorse, hawthorn, blackthorn and other berried shrubs also colonise the area, often spread by birds.

Sea buckthorn *Hippophae rhamnoides*

Sea buckthorn is now common in Lancashire on the dunes at Ainsdale and St Annes. It was originally introduced from the east coast as an experiment in dune stabilisation. It has spread rapidly and its spiny stems and suckering habit have created dense thickets, forming a sanctuary for rabbits. The orange berries contrast beautifully with the grey-green foliage and form a useful food supply for birds in autumn. The birds in turn disperse the undigested seeds, aiding the plant's spread.

A number of plant species are associated with the areas surrounding the mouths of rabbit burrows, which are slightly richer in nutrients. These include nettles, the two species of dandelion already mentioned, ragwort and groundsel. Common storksbill (*Erodium cicutarium*), soft cranesbill (*Geranium molle*), ribwort plantain, bulbous buttercup

Rest harrow (*Ononis repens*).

Chicory (*Chichorum intybus*), close-up of flower being pollinated by a bumble bee. Other colour variants of the flower include dark blue and purple.

Evening primrose (*Oenothera erythrosepala*) – a dense stand of flowering specimens in early July.

Sea buckthorn (*Hippophae rhamnoides*) in fruit.

and annual poa also seem to have a preference for this situation.

Dune slacks

Dune slacks usually develop between dune ridges, either locally where blow outs have occurred or over greater distances, paralleling the dunes and extending up to a couple of hundred metres in width. It is said that Lord Street in Southport was developed along such a dune slack, the shops and buildings being built on the ridges. Dune slacks are particularly well developed on the western coasts of the British Isles. Many are just above the water table in summer, but from October to April may be submerged to varying depths. The extensive slacks on the sand dunes of North Walney Island near Barrow-in-Furness were well submerged even in the drought of 1984.

Rainfall dissolves limy material from the surrounding dunes and this drains into the slacks, giving rise to a rich fen vegetation including great reedmace, water horsetail, various aquatic sedges and branched burr reed. Water plantain grows extensively on slacks, while in areas of open water rafts of broad-leaved pondweed (*Potamogeton natans*) form a leafy covering. These plants promote the rapid accumulation of partially decayed organic material, and in such places the beautiful pink and white flowers of buckbean, now often called bogbean (*Menyanthes trifoliata*), can be seen in early June accompanied by its decorative trifoliate leaves.

Where the land rises slightly or the water table is somewhat lower, marsh plants like the lovely purple loosestrife (*Lythrum salicaria*) occur. Almost a metre (3 feet) tall and often dominating the vegetation, it grows among water mint, marsh marigold, marsh pennywort and ladies smock (*Cardamine pratensis*). In slightly drier places creeping willow (*Salix repens*) has also established itself. It dominates great areas of both slack and slope in the dunes of Ainsdale and St Annes in Lancashire. It extends in almost pure stands right across the slacks, giving way in deeper water to the marsh and fen vegetation described above. Creeping willow, like marram grass, is a fast-growing species and can keep pace with some deposition of blown sand. It produces lots of leaf litter, too, forming ideal conditions for the local development of wintergreen (*Pyrola rotundifolia*). This rare, elegant plant stands 15 to 20cm (6–8 inches) above a rosette of glossy, dark green, round leaves and bears a column of six to eight pure white flowers, each of which has a long recurved style protruding beyond the petals.

Associated with the willow are groups of damp grassland and marsh species. These include magnificent orchids like the marsh helleborine (*Epipactis palustre*) with its nodding white flowers and purple-flowered ones such as the fen orchid (*Dacrylorhiza praetimissa*), the early marsh orchid (*D. incarnata*) and the northern fen orchid (*D. purpurella*). The lovely pink-flowered bog

Grass of Parnassus (*Parnassia palustris*) – a stunted form found on the sand dunes of south-west Lancashire.

pimpernel forms a delicate carpet in June and is followed in July by the pretty white-flowered Grass of Parnassus, all of 20cm (8 inches) in height.

Dune heath

As the dunes age, particularly in situations where the calcium carbonate content was originally low, there is a tendency for the dune soil to become rather acidic. Humus accumulates and the dunes become colonised by acid-loving (acidiphilous) species such as common heather or ling (*Calluna vulgaris*) and bell heather (*Erica cinerea*). These two plants dominate the vegetation but among them occur many plants typical of moorland or heath, such as tormentil, heath bedstraw, sheep's sorrel, field woodrush and heath milk-wort. Bilberry, harebell and cross-leaved heath (*Erica tetralix*) are sometimes found and bracken may dominate locally.

In conclusion, it can be said that a sand dune system provides a great variety of conditions, from arid to wet and from strongly alkaline to very acidic. Its development includes habitats ranging from bare sand with the occasional plant to a closed vegetation with a well-developed shrub vegetation. It is not surprising that such areas are rich in plant species. The range of habitat and plant form also means that a variety of niches are available for colonisation by animals. These include a wide variety of insects and molluscs, amphibians, reptiles, birds and mammals.

Animal life

Banded snail *Cepaea nemoralis*

The large amount of broken sea shells and vegetation in sand dunes provides raw material for shell-building and a regular food supply for land snails. These are most frequently found in semi-mobile and permanent dunes and one of the commonest, most easily seen and most interesting is the banded snail. Its shell has a range of ground colours that are genetically determined, so that brown is dominant to pink which is dominant to yellow-green. The number of bands in the shell is also genetically controlled; bandless is dominant to banded, and an animal may have from one to five bands. The ground colour and banding camouflages the animal from predators, its effectiveness being determined by season and the colour of background vegetation. Thus a brown-coloured shell is less easily seen against shrivelled brown vegetation in a dry summer or in autumn, while green-yellow shells provide more effective camouflage in spring when the grass is green.

One way of assessing the survival value of this camouflage is to find a thrush's anvil. Thrushes roost, nest and breed in dune scrub and take snails as food items. The bird holds the snail in its beak and breaks it on a flat stone or hard patch of sand (the anvil) to get at the soft flesh inside. If the shell fragments are collected and the colours and patterns checked against those of the snail population in the surrounding area, the colour and pattern represented least frequently at the anvil will be the form best fitted to survive in those surroundings at that time. Regular sampling of area and anvil should be undertaken, as the forms represented in both may change with the season. Studies of this kind reveal much about the nature of natural selection and predation pressure. It is common to think of slugs and snails as being happiest in moist weather. These conditions do occur on dunes, especially in spring and autumn when the snails are most active. When dry conditions prevail, they seal themselves by their shell aperture to vegetation.

Insects

A whole range of arthropods, particularly insects, are common to the dunes. Mosquito-like forms complete their life-cycles in the slacks and a variety of solitary wasps and bees tunnel into sand banks to raise their broods.

Opposite Buckbean (*Menyanthes trifoliata*) – a plant of more organically rich waters of dune slacks.

Above Banded snail (*Cepaea nemoralis*) – a collection of one to five banded forms of both the yellow-green and brown-pink ground colour types.

Bumble bees are in evidence, especially in spring and summer, and all these insects are important pollinators.

The butterflies and moths are perhaps the most interesting and, as modern agricultural methods have destroyed both the food plants and habitats previously available elsewhere, sand dunes now often provide the best habitat for many species.

Puss moth *Cerura vinula*

Puss moth caterpillars are found on poplars and willows in July and August. They are bright green in colour, with a broad, yellow-edged, purple-brown band on their backs. The abdomen is extended into a long tail, which is brought forward over the head when the animal is threatened, making the creature look quite fearsome and acting as a warning display to potential predators. Its cocoon is beautifully camouflaged by the bark and leaf fragments worked into the silken threads. The moth is on the wing in May and June.

Cinnabar moth *Callimorpha jacobaeae*

The caterpillars of the cinnabar moth, with their typical black and orange or yellow bands, are common on ragwort. The striking colours provide a warning to predators of their distasteful flavour and increase the chances of survival. This is a good example of what geneticists call 'aposematic coloration'.

Larvae of a cinnabar moth (*Callimorpha jacobaeae*) on ragwort.

The name 'cinnabar' refers to the almost vermilion colour of the hind wings of the adult, which is on the wing in May and June.

Six spot burnet

Sygaena fillipendulae

Although by no means confined to dune systems, this delightful red and blackish-green moth with six crimson spots on each forewing is a typical member of the dune fauna. The hairy greenish caterpillar bears black markings and yellow spots and feeds on plants such as trefoils, clover and kidney vetch. It builds a cocoon on marram or ribwort plantain stems in late June. This is at first transparent, but later becomes opaque. The moth hatches in July and the black pupal case partially emerges from the cocoon in the process.

Butterflies common on the dunes include the meadow brown, gatekeeper, small heath, common blue, wall brown, small tortoiseshell, red admiral and painted lady.

Common blue *Polyomatus icarus*

The common blue is so characteristic of dunes as to merit further description. The adult butterfly is on the wing from May to September. The male is blue, tinged with violet or mauve, the wings narrowly edged with black. The female, however, is usually brown with some blue scales on the basal areas of the wings. The eggs are usually laid on birdsfoot trefoil or rest harrow and produce green caterpillars covered with short brown hairs. The head is black and glossy. The caterpillars are found after hibernation in April and as a second brood in June and July.

Small tortoiseshell *Vanessa urticae*

As its scientific name implies, the eggs of the small tortoiseshell are laid under the terminal leaves of nettles (*Urtica dioica*), which provide food for the caterpillar. This is yellowish with black speckles and a black line running down its back, and is covered with short hairs. There are two broods a year, one in June and the other in August and September. At least some of the adults from the second brood hibernate and reappear early in spring, disproving the idea that butterflies only live for a day.

Amphibians

The common frog, common toad and common newt all inhabit dune slacks, where insect larvae and adults provide an ample food supply. The water is an ideal medium for copulation, egg-laying and maturation of the young.

Natterjack toad *Bufo calamita*

The natterjack toad is especially associated with coastal situations in Britain, where it is at the northern edge of its range. Among other locations it can be found on the dune systems at Ainsdale in Lancashire and at Braunton Burrows in Devon. At 7 to 8cm (3 inches) the male is about 2·5cm (1 inch) shorter than its mate. Both have brown skin

Small tortoiseshell (*Vanessa urticae*) feeding on creeping thistle.

Natterjack toad (*Bufo calamita*). As its habitat is destroyed, it is becoming less common.

with a thin yellow line down the centre of their backs. Having short hind limbs, the natterjack runs rather than jumps. It survives hot days in summer and inactive periods in winter in a burrow which it excavates from the sand. It is easily recognisable at dusk in the breeding season from the ratchet-like croak which it emits in bursts one or two seconds long. It lays its eggs in strings in the water of the dune slacks, showing a preference for brackish conditions. They hatch quickly and the metamorphosis from tadpole to miniature adult takes place within six weeks. This maturation is more rapid than in most amphibians and may be an adaptation to the rapid drying out of slack pools in summer. In areas where housing developments or other causes have altered the local water table, the natterjack toad sometimes lays eggs in pools which dry out before the tadpoles mature.

Left Six-spot burnet moth (*Zygaena filipendula*). Two adults drying out, having left the pupal cases (exuvia) and newly emerged from their cocoons.

Below Common blue (*Polyommatus icarus*), male with open wings.

This interference with breeding grounds and the reduction in the area and number of habitats since the Second World War now threaten its survival in Britain.

Reptiles

Both the viviparous lizard and the sand lizard are found on coastal sand dunes in Britain, but while the former is generally distributed throughout the country the latter is limited to the Formby/Ainsdale reserve in Lancashire and a few other sites, such as the Dorset downs and dunes in Hampshire and the Isle of Wight.

Viviparous lizard *Lacerta vivipara*

Up to 6·5cm (2½ inches) long from snout to vent and with a tail of up to twice that length, this short-legged lizard is a dull brown colour, often with scattered light or dark spots, which are more pronounced in the male. The females sometimes bear a dark vertebral stripe. I have found the viviparous lizard most frequently among creeping willow, where the greyish brown leaf litter and sand provide a background against which it is not easily seen. When camouflage fails and it is caught by bird or mammal predators it can shed its tail without harm (a process called autotomy) and sometimes escapes to grow a new one – a useful survival strategy not found in animals evolutionarily more advanced than reptiles. The viviparous lizard feeds predominantly on invertebrates and, as its name implies, gives birth to fully-formed young, although some Continental populations lay eggs.

Sand lizard *Lacerta agilis*

The adult sand lizard is slightly larger than its viviparous relative, measuring about 9cm (3½ inches) from snout to vent, with a tail of about 14cm (5½ inches). The green on the flanks of the male, particularly in the breeding season, is another distinguishing feature. However, I have only found sand lizards on open sand near patches of vegetation on the drier semi-mobile dunes, quite different from the willow litter where viviparous lizards are usually found. So in sand dune systems perhaps there is some habitat separation too. The female lays from eight to ten eggs measuring 10 by 30mm (²/₅ by 1¼ inches) in a hole excavated in the sand. They hatch in eight to ten weeks, depending upon temperature. I have often come across the bleached, papery egg cases with one end broken open and hope they represent breeding success, since, like the natterjack toad, the sand lizard is now a threatened species in England and Wales.

Birds

In late spring a walk of two or three hundred yards inland will take you into the high yellow dunes and out of earshot of the sea. Lie with closed eyes on a warm dune bank and a variety of birdsong will assail your ears. Most obvious is the tune of the skylark (*Alauda arvensis*) as she rises in the air. The drier slacks provide an ideal nesting site for this bird, and the insect life an abundant source of food. The high-pitched notes of the swift (*Apus apus*) and swallow (*Hirundo rustica*) can also be heard, temporary visitors hawking through the harvest of airborne insects. The meadow pipit (*Anthus pratensis*), with its undulating flight, is also there and in the wetter slacks the reed bunting (*Emberiza schoeniclus*) perches on low willow branches. From the nearby shoots of sea buckthorn, sedge warblers (*Acrocephalus schoenobanus*) look on. Here and there on the tops of wind-trimmed gorse the beautiful male stonechat (*Saxicola torquata*), with its black head, white collar and lovely reddish breast, makes the sound that defines its territory, while elsewhere the mellifluous notes of the equally beautiful linnet (*Acanthis cannabina*) can be heard. The yellowhammer (*Emberiza citrinella*) gives its 'little-bit-of-bread-and-no-cheese', and among the alder

Sand lizards (*Lacerta agilis*) – like the natterjack toad, a threatened species in England and Wales.

scrub wrens (*Troglodytes troglodytes*), robins (*Erithacus rubecula*) and dunnocks (*Prunella modularis*) feast on the insect food on leaves and twigs, while treecreepers (*Certhia familiaris*) and great spotted woodpeckers (*Dendrocopas major*) probe the bark with beak and tongue. Thrushes dart out from the shrub cover to search for insects, worms and, of course, the banded snail. But now the blackbird emits his warning note – perhaps a hunting kestrel lurks nearby and the birdsong changes. In late autumn those winter migrant thrushes, the fieldfare and redwing, gorge themselves on the fruit of sea buckthorn, hawthorn and sloe.

On South Walney, near Barrow, the dunes lack much of the scrub cover of other dune areas and there is an extensive gullery of around 80,000 herring and lesser black-backed gulls (*Larus fuscus*). About a dozen pairs of great black-backed gulls (*Larus marinus*) are also present and 800 pairs of eider ducks (*Somateria mollissima*) benefit from the protection of the massed flocks of gulls, occupying their most southerly nesting site on the west

coast of Britain. Mallard and shelduck also breed here, and the little owl reaches the northern limit of its distribution.

The group of seven islands, of which Walney is the largest, has been a breeding ground for sea birds for centuries and the name Foulney (Bird Island) indicates that in the tenth and eleventh centuries sea birds bred there, while the part of the shore called Maw Flat refers to the 'sea maws' or gulls which nested there.

Herring gull *Larus argentatus*

The herring gull is a resident species in Britain. During their breeding season on Walney small piles of broken mussel shells, cockle shells and fish bones, or a mixture of all three, appear. These are the regurgitated remains of gull meals discharged from the crop as pellets similar to those produced by birds of prey, such as kestrels or owls.

Out of the gulls' breeding season Walney is relatively tranquil and the herring gulls are dispersed around the coastal towns and resorts of Lancashire and Cumbria. A few start to return in December, but the numbers only really build up in late February and March. The male birds eventually occupy particular pieces of ground as their territory and advertise this fact to potential trespassers by posturing in a highly vocal way. This behaviour has been investigated by Tinbergen (*see* bibliography). A posture known as the 'upright position' (the neck is held vertically and the bill may be positioned horizontally or slightly downwards, while the wings are held away from the body) warns off adventurers in boundary disputes. Another advertisement of territorial aggression is achieved by the 'oblique long call'. The gull points its head obliquely forwards and slightly up, emitting a single hoarse call, then the head is jerked down and a couple of muffled, high-pitched calls are produced. The sequence is completed by throwing back the head – the bill describing an arc of 180 degrees – and a series of loud calls, made as the bill returns to the horizontal position.

By a series of vocal and postural interactions the male accepts a female onto his patch and eventually mates with her. Various pieces of behaviour now strengthen their pair-bonding and they jointly build their nest. Herring gulls seem to show a preference for nest-building in open areas, while lesser black-backed gulls opt for taller, thicker grass. The privacy provided by the thicker grass allows nests to be sited closer together.

The nest usually contains a maximum of three eggs and, while the normal colour consists of blackish-brown splashes on an olive-brown ground colour, I have seen unspotted bluey-green eggs and a great range of patterns and colour within a clutch. Herring gulls are cannibals and will often eat an egg from an unguarded nest, or even a neighbour's chick. The incubation period is about twenty-eight days. Herring gulls start incubation as soon as the first egg is laid, so that the hatch is staggered and in times of food shortage the younger, weaker birds, unable to compete for food, may die. This adaptation ensures that at least some breeding success is achieved in hard times, and is not uncommon in other species.

Experiments

Providing that it meets with the warden's approval and if you are willing to risk being attacked by gulls, a great deal of interesting information can be gathered about these birds and their nests using very little equipment. It is perhaps best to compare the herring gull and the lesser black-backed gull in any investigation. Binoculars and a field notebook are essential for any ornithologist and to compare egg sizes a ruler with a metric scale, a spring balance provided with a sling to hold the egg and a pair of callipers are all the extra equipment needed. Use your binoculars from a distance to establish which species are nesting in the area. Approach quietly, examine the eggs, measure the length and breadth and weigh each one carefully, ensuring that they are replaced exactly in their original position. A minimum of 100 eggs of each species should be sampled.

Gulls have eggs which are well camouflaged. However, on hatching, the white interior and sharp edge of the broken shell make the rest of the nest site more obvious to predators, so gulls, like most other birds, remove such shell material at the earliest opportunity. An experiment using half shells of hens' eggs (available in quantity from any mass catering establishment) with the outsides initially painted a uniform olive-brown involves setting the shells edge uppermost both in the nests themselves and at a distance of 10cm, 20cm, 30cm and so on from each of the nests. For the experiments to be statistically valid, a sample of at least twenty replicates per treatment should be carried out and the egg shells should be of uniform size. the number of egg shells required is primarily determined by the number of treatments the investigator wishes to undertake; however, 200 egg shells would not seem to be excessive. The aim of the experiment is to find out the maximum distance at which the gull feels it necessary to remove the eggshell.

As gulls nest in colonies, ensure that the

Herring gull (*Larus argentatus*) on nest.

note the differences, if any, in the nesting
material used in each species.

nest or gull under investigation is far enough
away from adjacent nests to avoid interference
and that only one species of gull is being considered at a time. (On Walney Island near
Barrow-in-Furness both herring gulls and
lesser black-backed gulls nest together.) As
sand dunes are often windy places, it is
important to ensure that the shells will not be
blown from their intended locations.

All these factors mean that the experiments
need to be under constant observation, either
from a hide or a distant dune ridge. Binoculars
are essential in either case.

Variations of this experiment include re-
peating it with the broken shell edge hidden.
Also, the response of the gulls to eggs painted
in different primary colours (yellow, red,
blue) can be investigated in a similar way.

Finally, measure the inside and outside
diameters of the nests to see if they relate to
nest density in both tall and short grass and

Black-headed gull *Larus ridibundus*

Sand dune systems are popular with a wide
variety of birds, many of which have been
noted above. The black-headed gull is no exception. Less aggressive than the herring gull,
it has been ousted from many coastal breeding
sites and has moved into moorland areas in
order to breed.

Like the herring gull, pairs of birds hold
territory within the colony and their behaviour patterns are, at least in principle, similar.
Nevertheless, individuals seem to work for
the overall benefit of the colony. Often the
sky may appear to have only one black-headed
gull on the wing, but as soon as it spies a food
source (say, worms in freshly turned earth at
ploughing time) it starts to call and very
quickly many other birds of the species appear
as if from nowhere. Black-headed gulls also
act together in the defence of their colony. For

Black-headed gull (*Larus ridibundus*).

teeth (the incisors) of mice, voles, rabbits and hares are shaped like chisels so that they can gnaw away at roots or nibble grass. This subjects them to great wear and tear, but unlike our teeth they continue to grow and so are unaffected.

Analysis of the faecal pellets of rabbits has shown that in some dune systems red fescue is the most popular grass, while Yorkshire fog, bent grass and, less popularly, marram grass are also eaten. Scientists know this because plant species have characteristic patterns of cells, stomata and hairs in the outer skin or epidermis of their leaves. These epidermi can often be isolated from faecal pellets by boiling three pellets in 5ml (one teaspoonful) of concentrated nitric acid in a boiling water bath. The pellets fragment in three to six minutes, and on cooling 55ml (1¼ fluid ounces) of a preserving solution made up of equal parts of 30 per cent glycerine and formol-acetic-alcohol is added. A 5ml sample is transferred in a wide-mouthed dropper to a small sample-tube to which a drop of gentian violet is added. Drops containing stained suspended leaf fragments are microscopically examined using a × 100 magnification for identification. If you have the facilities and skill to do this and wish to check the food preferences of the rabbits in your local dunes, a reference collection of local plant leaf material is invaluable.

Rats may also be present in dunes, as well as stoats, weasels and even polecats. All will take eggs and young birds for food. The last three species mentioned will also take young rabbits, which scream like human babies when a stoat is making its kill. This is quite disturbing, but carnivores only take the weak and inferior animals of a species and thus ensure that the population is kept fit and under control.

Foxes commonly frequent dune systems. If you are not fortunate enough to see one, you can examine the moister areas around the slacks and look for their footprints.

example, if a crow flies over the breeding site it is immediately mobbed and the attacking gulls often force the luckless bird to the ground.

Birds of prey

Birds of prey are often found on sand dunes and include the short-eared owl (*Asio flammeus*) and the kestrel (*Falco tinnunculus*). Peregrine falcons (*Falco peregrinus*) may also sometimes be seen hunting overhead.

Mammals

Among the mammals that inhabit sand dunes are rabbits, field voles, field mice and shrews. The teeth of shrews and of some hedgehogs are pointed, an adaptation which enables them to cope with insects and invertebrates generally, so that they can benefit from the abundant food supply. In contrast, the front

6 CONSERVATION

During the twentieth century the coastline of Britain has been transformed. Two world wars led to the presence of mined beaches, concrete 'pill boxes', tank traps and barbed wire barriers on various parts of the coast. Then the need to develop coastal refineries and oil-handling facilities during the Second World War was intensified in the post-war years, when a car for every family became the aim of the motor manufacturers. At the same time the explosion in the plastics and chemical industries brought about further industrialisation of our coastline. The post-war years also saw the extensive development of retirement bungalows on the coast, often bought by people who had enjoyed seaside holidays between the wars.

Since the Second World War there has been a progressive reduction in working hours, with more free weekends and a minimum of three weeks annual holiday for most by the late 1960s. Sunbathing, walking, swimming, horse riding, water skiing, sailing, sea angling, surf boarding and sand yachting have all become popular seaside activities and recent years have seen a tremendous increase in the development of coastal caravan parks and the construction of marinas, swimming pools and golf courses.

Indeed, one may well wonder if there is any unspoilt coastline left at all. Thanks to the National Trust, the answer is yes. In May 1963 the National Trust launched Enterprise Neptune, the most ambitious conservation project ever launched in Britain. Its aim was to highlight the need to preserve the coastline and to acquire, either by gift or purchase, the remaining 900 miles of unspoilt coast in England, Wales and Northern Ireland. The initial appeal was to raise £2 million from both the government and by public subscription. The appeal was so successful that by 1984–5 £7 million had been raised and 450 miles of the desired coastline purchased.

On 23 April 1985 Enterprise Neptune was relaunched since pressures on the remaining coastline had significantly increased and become more immediate than in 1963, including demands for housing and leisure developments. However, the more serious threat was and still is the pollution of coast and shore by industrial effluents and sewage and the development of nuclear power stations and oil wells.

The extraction of oil is particularly pertinent as only recently Dorset County Council has given British Petroleum permission to drill for oil on Fursey Island in Poole Harbour – land owned by the National Trust – despite strong opposition from conservation bodies. The decision was even more surprising in that the area, which includes Poole Harbour and the whole of the Purbecks, was awarded a European prize for conservation in 1984. At the time of writing, the National Trust is awaiting the result of an appeal to the Secretary of State for the Environment to withdraw drilling permission.

In the twentieth century other problems of coastal conservation relating to individual species require consideration. For example, issues such as the impact of the grey seal population on salmon fisheries and the effects of oystercatcher predation on cockle beds have arisen as a result of competition with man for a common food resource.

Competition between man and wildlife

The oystercatcher and man

The oystercatcher feeds on several kinds of intertidal invertebrates, of which the edible mussel, the common cockle and the Baltic tellin are the most important. During the 1960s and 1970s considerable controversy arose over the effect of oystercatcher predation on the stocks of commercial shellfish fisheries at the Burry inlet in South Wales. Feeling on the part of the fishery was so strong that the Ministry of Agriculture gave permission to cull 11,000 oystercatchers, of which 7,000 were killed in 1973. Members of the RSPB and conservationists in general were greatly concerned about the culling, especially since it appeared to have been permitted for reasons of political expediency, and only limited scientific data was available regarding the likely effects.

In 1976 the Institute of Terrestrial Ecology, a branch of the National Environmental Research Council, initiated a research programme in which the nature of oystercatcher predation on intertidal shellfish was investigated. It was found that in the Wash oystercatchers showed a preference for shellfish of a particular size, irrespective of numbers, and took other shellfish in large numbers only when the preferred ones were scarce. Their preference was for large Baltic tellins of about 12 to 14mm (½ inch) and medium-sized cockles of 25 to 30mm (1–1⅕ inches).

It was also shown that the density of the oystercatcher population appeared to increase when more cockles were available. However, it was suggested that above a certain density the oystercatchers vied with one another to such an extent that the less aggressive birds would retire to feeding grounds where lower shellfish densities occurred, thus reducing the pressure on the more densely populated feeding grounds.

The conclusion based on previous research that oystercatchers took 90 per cent of the second year cockles (the commercially favoured size) was shown to be an over-estimate and that a figure of between 30 and 47 per cent was more likely. It is admitted that oystercatchers favour areas also used as commercial cockle grounds. However, the removal of birds by culling does not reduce predation – since birds from other localities replace them, making the cull ineffective.

Before such an extreme measure as culling is taken, it must therefore be demonstrated that it will be effective, that it will be carried out for the right reasons and that it will only be undertaken after full scientific evaluation, thus providing good conservation. In this way scientific research can help prevent the extermination of species competing with man.

The grey seal and salmon fisheries

The largest British mammal, the grey seal, (*Halichoerus grypus*), was in danger of extinction when the first Grey Seals Protection Act was passed in 1914, at which time their numbers were estimated to be as low as 500. By 1947 they had increased to such an extent that the grey seal had earned the reputation of being a pest in the salmon fisheries along the east coast of Scotland. As a result of a three-year research programme financed by the government, a report was published in 1963 which evaluated the situation. The world population of grey seals was then estimated to be about 46,000, of which 78 per cent was distributed around the British Isles. It was shown that while seals take a variety of food, the consumption of salmon was indeed fairly high and that many salmon are bitten by seals, making them unfit to eat. Fishermen claimed that 10 per cent of all nets are damaged by seals and that large numbers of fish escape through torn nets.

Meanwhile, in 1959 a cull of young seals (moulters) on the Farnes caused a public outcry. As a result, the landowners – the

Durdle Dor – the rock has eroded to form an arch which can be seen from the Dorset Coastal path.

National Trust – refused permission for further culls. However, this no culling policy allowed the local grey seal population to increase greatly so that by 1970 the Farnes breeding rookeries had become overcrowded, pup mortality had risen to a high level because of increased aggressiveness in the breeding cows (also thought to be caused by overcrowding) and habitat destruction was occurring to the detriment of both the seal and the Farnes sea bird population. A management plan prepared for the Farnes in 1971 proposed a 50 per cent reduction of the grey seal breeding population from 2,000 to 1,000 which was to occur over three years.

The most effective method of population control is by culling adult cows, since if bulls dominating rookeries are killed they are soon replaced, while seal pup culling seems simply to constitute an alternative to their natural

high mortality rate and so does not materially affect the seal population.

It can, therefore, be seen that controlled culling of the grey seal population may not only help the salmon fisheries but may even benefit the species itself. The main essential is to have a good information base on which to plan the management of the seal population. The introduction of the Seals Act of 1970 seems to provide for this.

Exotic species

The accidental import or development of exotic species has brought about significant modification of our beaches and coasts. Four species which are fairly well documented are described below.

Rice grass *Spartina × townsendii*

As mentioned in Chapter 4, rice grass is a hybrid between European cord grass (*S. maritima*) and an imported species, American cord grass (*S. alterniflora*), and was first recorded in 1870 in Southampton Water.

Grey seal (*Halichoerus grippus*) pup, Bass Rock, North Berwick.

Like many hybrids, it shows much greater vigour than either of its parents and its capacity to grow in and to stabilise mobile mud has led to the spread of this plant along our coasts. There is some evidence that it has been spread artificially, for as mud accumulates and the grass is established as a continuous sward it provides grazing for sheep and increases both the land area and stock-carrying capacity of coastal farms.

Mud that previously was scoured away by tidal currents now tends to stay. As a result, glasswort, a typical pioneer coloniser of salt marshes and estuaries with a preference for more sandy conditions, is less able to compete and is displaced by rice grass. Changes in the salt marsh fauna may also have taken place. For example, the crustacean *Corophium arenaria*, which also prefers sandy conditions, may have been replaced by the mud-loving *C. volutator*.

Rice grass causing mud accumulation, Borth salt marsh, Aberystwyth.

Japanese seaweed
Sargassum muticum

Japanese seaweed, which grows up to 8m (26 feet) in length, was first noted in this country at Bembridge in the Isle of Wight in 1973. Since then it has established itself and has spread so rapidly that by 1983 it occupied sites from Eastbourne in Sussex to the Lizard Peninsular in Cornwall. The invasion of Japanese seaweed has provoked something of an international furore, since the French blame the English and the English the French for its importation. The French argue that it was imported with mature oysters as packing material at Poole in Dorset, while the English blame its importation on young oysters and oyster spat (larval oysters) introduced into the oyster beds near Cherbourg. Dr Steve Morrell (*see* bibliography) favours the latter view, since the plant was not recorded at Poole until 1978.

But why all the fuss? What is an extra seaweed or two along our extensive coastline? One problem is that when Japanese seaweed grows on oyster shells the masses of air bladders float the oysters to the surface and ruin the fishery. Another is that the long tangles of fronds cause problems for swimmers, damage fishermen's nets and foul boat propellers and cooling intakes. Last but not least, there is evidence that Japanese seaweed has adversely affected native seaweeds on the Pacific coast of North America and there is concern over its impact upon the unique marine community at Bembridge, which is scheduled as a Site of Special Scientific Interest by the Nature Conservancy Council.

So great is the concern that several attempts have been made to eradicate the seaweed by digging it out and burning it. However, as the plant can live floating in the sea and can also survive in salt marsh mud, it seems that these efforts are likely to be in vain. In consolation, it has been found that where Japanese seaweed has established itself in areas of the shore previously regarded as fairly barren it provides cover and food for a range of crabs and crustaceans and for the fishes that feed on them. As a result, anglers and commercial eel fishermen in Langstone Harbour, near Portsmouth, are now making better catches than before.

Slipper limpet *Crepidula fornicata*

Another invader from North America when Britain's prestige as a maritime nation was at its height was the slipper limpet. This univalve mollusc first appeared in the 1880s and by the 1950s had spread from the Humber all around the south coast to Devon. Like another invader from North America, the oyster drill (*Urosalpinx cinerea*), it has now become a serious pest of oyster beds, although unlike the oyster drill I have not found it on the north-western shores of Britain.

Slipper limpets live in chains of seven to nine animals, each settling on the back of another. With advancing age the animals undergo a sex change – and so the lowermost limpet is always female, the middle ones of intermediate sex and the uppermost ones smaller, younger males.

A plankton feeder, the slipper limpet does not attack the oyster itself, but is damaging in that it reproduces prolificly and competes with the oyster for food and space.

Acorn barnacle *Elminius modestus*

A fourth invader of our shores is a species of acorn barnacle which became established on the south coast in the Second World War. A native of Australasia, its tolerance of temperature variations and desiccation match those of our native acorn barnacles (*see* Chapter 2), while a preference for brackish conditions has favoured its establishment in harbours and estuaries at the expense of the British species. It is easily distinguished by having four, as opposed to six, wall plates. Its successful establishment in this country is probably due at least in part to its extended breeding season (April to November), compared with a period

Empty shells of the slipper limpet (*Crepidula fornicata*).

of six weeks, at a temperature of 10°C with less than twelve hours of daylight, for *Balanus balanoides* and a few weeks at a temperature above 15°C for the *Chthamalus stellatus*. It is also much less critical in its requirements for maturation and fertilisation.

The coast as a human amenity

The availability of self-catering flats, camp sites and caravan parks has been a boon for the less wealthy and for those who prefer a more relaxed holiday to a fixed hotel routine. What could be more delightful than the sun streaming in through the tent flap early in the morning with the birds singing and one's soul on the very edge of nature's wilderness?

However, this idyllic situation is only realised where camp and caravan sites have been the subject of careful planning and environmental control, for the location and appearance of such places often have more to do with profit than with aesthetic considerations. But this is not always the case. For example, there is a beautiful caravan site at Arnside in north Lancashire. The caravans are carefully positioned among conifers and other trees, and the whole site is in no way offensive to the landscape, when seen from either nearby or from a distance. What a contrast to those sites where caravans are packed in rows at densities that no planning officer would allow in permanent housing schemes. Vigilance is essential to ensure good environmental planning, coupled with a willingness to apply pressure on MPs and local councillors and to provide support for county naturalists' trusts and similar organisations.

Another problem is access to beaches. Beach visits often involve a car journey with all the family paraphernalia. The provision of car-parks is, therefore, often essential. Car-

Rice grass (*Spartina × townsendii*) – close-up showing stigmas of flowers.

Downs Way, parts of which extend along the coast, care has been taken not only to avoid areas where birds need to be left undisturbed but also to cater for treading pressure, which can lead to path erosion if alternative routes are not provided – considerations that barely enter the thoughts of the average tourist or carefree holidaymaker.

Pollution of the shore

Like most other natural environments in Great Britain, our beaches and coasts have suffered from pollution created by human activities.

Sewage and other discharges

Immediately after the Second World War the relatively low sewage output from coastal towns was easily dispersed by tidal currents. Now, however, the considerable increase in the population of some coastal areas, boosted even further in the holiday season, has raised the volume and strength of sewage discharge to such an extent that treatment facilities are often less than adequate. A walk on some beaches at low tide can be quite disgusting, with apparently untreated discharge from sewage pipes bobbing about on the gently lapping waves and sanitary towels frequently visible among the flotsam and jetsam washed up by the last high tide.

This is the visible problem. Yet it is perhaps less insidious than the high coliform bacteria count that occurs on the beaches of some coastal towns. Coliform bacteria, though not in themselves harmful, are found in the human gut and are discharged with faeces, so their presence in sea water and on beaches is an indication of the level of sewage contamination and reflects a potential health hazard to human beings. But the impact on native beach organisms is quite different, for the enriching effect of the sewage does not bring about oxygen-deficient conditions in the sea as it does in fresh water, since strong wave action maintains high oxygen concentrations. Indeed,

parks also make it possible to regulate the numbers of people on a beach and protect beaches from indiscriminate parking, which can be extremely damaging to wildlife. On a barrier beach in south-east Carolina, for example, compaction caused by driving over sand dunes and grassland reduced the vegetated area considerably and led to extensive erosion. So the parking fee which we sometimes resent may well be a contribution to preserving a better environment and a reflection of good planning too.

One way to avoid excessive densities and to enable lovers of the coast to enjoy the scenery is to provide coastal walks. The Countryside Commission has done a splendid job in planning walks which have suitable stopping points either for a few hours' stroll or for back-packers who wish to cover a greater distance. In planning coastal walks such as the South-West Coastal Path and the Pembrokeshire Coastal Path, and long-distance routes such as the Cleveland Way and the South

Above Part of the coastal section of the Yorkshire National Park walk near Robin Hood's Bay, Scarborough, Yorkshire.

Below Conservation volunteers planting marram grass to prevent sand dune erosion. They are removing growing marram and replanting the roots in specially prepared trenches.

such enrichment acts as a stimulus to the food chains of the shore organisms; increased growth rates as well as higher numerical concentrations of animals close to sewage outlets provide evidence of this. For example, the discharge of vegetable waste on the Lincolnshire coast is said to be positively beneficial to mussel growth there, while domestic waste has led to increased productivity in intertidal communities on certain rocky shores.

Chemical pollution

It is difficult to find any aesthetic pleasure in refinery installations based on the coast, or anywhere else, although we would soon complain if there was no petrol for our cars. However, the discharge of chemicals into the sea occurs in such a way as to bring about considerable dilution, so it is claimed that little damage can be detected beyond a few hundred yards from the outlet pipes. A study by S. Petpiroon and B. Dicks (*see* bibliography) on the environmental impact of refinery effluent at Milford Haven in Pembrokeshire supports this view. Their study, which considers records over the twenty-one years between 1969 and 1981, shows that the effects of the discharge were limited to within 200m (650 feet) of the discharge point. Nevertheless, both the limpet and periwinkle populations at Milford Haven have suffered and their absence or reduction in numbers has led to a corresponding increase in the abundance of fucoid seaweeds on which they graze. In addition a reduction in the barnacle population has been noted. This was thought to be due to the inhibition of larval settlement, partly as a result of the low salinity created by the effluent and partly because of its burden of oil and other constituents. However, effluent quality improvements in the early 1970s, which included a reduction of maximum oil content from fifty to twenty-five parts per million to meet new water authority regulations, do not seem to have brought about any biological changes in the affected area – though, since some of the effects were thought to be due to the reduced salinity of the effluent rather than to its chemical content, this was to be expected. In conclusion the authors suggested that small volumes of relatively clean effluents from mainly air-cooled refineries discharged into areas with strong currents and wave action where dispersion is good rarely result in significant biological damage.

Oil pollution

No one who has had a new swimsuit ruined by oil smears is going to feel happy about the effect of oil pollution on our oceans and beaches. Still less happy are the armies of naturalists who are rightly both indignant and concerned when they read about thousands of birds being killed in the North Sea as a result of oil spills in Sullom Voe or the death of a significant percentage of the guillemot population on the Cornish coast due to oil spillage, like that from the *Torrey Canyon* in 1967.

The effects of these oil spills have been much studied since then, involving, as they do, financial and amenity considerations as well as the need to protect and manage environmental resources. Such spills often produce severe local damage, which is greatly exacerbated by the use of dispersant sprays. However, while the damage from the oil itself is usually short-lived, that caused by dispersant sprays is more lasting.

Spills from tanker accidents were considered to be responsible for only one to two per cent of the total oil input into the sea in 1975. However, the long-term pollution which results from the production, handling and refining of oil should be a matter of greater public concern, as should the behaviour of unscrupulous ships' captains who clean out their ballast tanks close to the shore.

Opposite Razorbills lying dead on a Lincolnshire beach, summer 1981.

Above The common limpet (*Patella vulgata*) grazes on seaweed. Experimental work shows it to be severely affected by chemical discharge.

Left Pinnacle rocks, Farne Islands.

Radioactive discharge

The harmful effects of radioactive substances on man are well known, as is the fact that they can cause death or damage not only to those exposed to radiation but also to the chromosomes of future generations. The way in which this damage occurs has been dealt with elsewhere by Christopher Lawrence (*see* bibliography). However, because radioactive wastes are discharged from shore to sea, as at Sellafield, and dumping still occurs in the sea, I make no apology for adding my own comments on this form of pollution. When the construction of nuclear power stations and processing plants (usually in coastal situations) is undertaken, the public is always given assurances that these installations are quite safe. The Three Mile Island accident in the

United States and those reported at Windscale (now Sellafield) in November 1982 and January 1984 clearly require us to consider further what is meant by 'safe'.

It may be that the risks associated with such accidents are acceptably low. It may, on the other hand, be the case that governments are willing to condone a certain level of human damage and environmental contamination in return for the economic advantages of nuclear energy. Moreover, advances in technology can give rise to events and processes that lie beyond the state of knowledge which exists when decisions to embark on nuclear projects are taken. The thirty-year period up to the mid-1960s saw a revision of the 'safe' figure for radiation dosage to one per cent of the figure previously accepted – which suggests that decisions regarding increased use of radioactive materials have been made in ignorance and that the implementation of such decisions should be delayed for a generation until more is known about their impact on our own health and the health of our children. Moreover, arguments justifying the need for nuclear energy as a replacement for fossil fuels are less persuasive now than they were in the 1960s if only because of the shrinking size of the country's industrial base and the availability of other forms of fuel.

If the level of investment in research into alternative technology equalled the amount spent on nuclear research, that in itself might well obviate the need for increased use of nuclear fuel. Indeed, the use of tidal power and solar energy is already yielding promising results both in this country and in France.

The ability of marine organisms to concentrate some elements to 100,000 times their concentration in sea water and the further concentrating effects of passing these materials up the food chains leading to man are said to be taken into consideration when calculating 'safe' levels for the release of radioactive material. However, when this claim is viewed against a local doctor's assertion that levels of

Windscale atomic power station.

leukaemia in children near Sellafield are well above the national average, that local fishmongers are reputed to buy their fish from the east coast and that 'beach unsafe' notices appear on Cumbrian beaches from time to time, then one cannot avoid the feeling that our environment is in the process of being irreversibly damaged – for once radioactive material is liberated into the environment it cannot be recovered.

The future

Our beaches and coasts have provided food and shelter ever since the end of the last ice age. Today they provide a living for some and an opportunity for enjoyment and renewal for many. That they are under threat as a resource for future generations is clear. It is the responsibility of the present adult population to exert pressure on the government and other relevant authorities and to give active support to the environmental lobby in order to preserve our heritage for our children's children.

FURTHER READING

Alvin, K.L., *The Observer's Book of Lichens* (Warne, 1977).

Arnold, E.N., Burton, J.A., and Ovenden, D.W., *A Field Guide to the Reptiles and Amphibians of Britain and Europe* (Collins, 1978).

Ballantine, W.J., 'A biologically defined exposure for the comparative description of rocky shores', *Field Studies*, vol. 1, no. 3 (1961).

Bannerman, D.A., and Lodge, G.E., *The Birds of the British Isles* (Oliver and Boyd, 1953).

Barnes, R.S.K., *Estuarine Biology* (Arnold, 1974).

Barrett, J., and Yonge, C.M., *Pocket Guide to the Seashore* (Collins, 1958).

Bolton, E.M., *Lichens for Vegetable Dyeing* (Studio Vista, 1969).

Bondfield, A.E., *Life in Sandy Shores*, Studies in Biology 89 (Arnold, 1978).

Brehaut, R.N., *Ecology of Rocky Shores*, Studies in Biology 139 (Arnold, 1982).

Campbell, A.C., and Nicholls, J., *Hamlyn Guide to the Seashore and Shallow Seas of Britain and Europe* (Hamlyn, 1976).

Chinery, M., *A Field Guide to the Insects of Britain* (Collins, 1972).

Clapham, A.R., Tutin, T.G., and Warburg, E.F., *Flora of the British Isles* (CUP, 1962).

Coverdale, N., 'Environmental Monitoring around Sellafield', *Country-Side*, vol. 25, no. 7 (1984).

Crothers, J., and Crothers, M., 'A key to the crabs and crab-like animals of British inshore waters', *Field Studies*, vol. 5, pp.753–806 (1983).

Ford, E.V., *How to Begin your Fieldwork (2), The Seashore* (Murray, 1964).

Freethy, R., *The Naturalist's Guide to the British Coastline* (David & Charles, 1982).

Godwin, Sir Harry, *The History of the British Flora* (CUP, 1956).

Gosse, P.H., *A Year at the Shore* (Dalby, Isbyster, 1877).

Goss-Custard, J.D., 'The winter predation of *Corophium volutator* by the redshank', *Ibis*, vol. 109, p.475 (1967).

Goss-Custard, J.D., McGrorty, S., and Reading, C., 'Oystercatchers and shellfish predator/prey studies', (Nature Conservancy Council, 1977).

Hardy, Sir Alistair, *The Open Sea (1), The World of Plankton* (Collins, 1956).

Hawksworth, D.L., 'A key to the lichens of the S. Devon coastal schists', *Field Studies*, vol. 5, part 2, pp.195–228 (1980).

Hawksworth, D.L., and Rose, F., *Lichens as Pollution Monitors*, Studies in Biology 66 (Arnold, 1976).

Hepburn, I., *Flowers of the Coast* (Collins, 1952).

Hewer, H.R., *British Seals* (Collins, 1974).

Hiscock, Sue, 'A field guide to British brown seaweeds (Phaeophyta)', *Field Studies*, vol. 5, part 1, pp. 1–44 (1979).

Lawrence, C.W., *Cellular Radiobiology*, Studies in Biology 30 (Arnold, 1971).

Lewis, J.R., *The Ecology of Rocky Shores* (English University Press, 1964).

Littler, M.M., and Murray, S.N., 'Influence of domestic wastes on energetic pathways in rocky intertidal communities', *Journal of Applied Ecology*, vol. 5, no. 2, pp.583–596 (1978).

McMillan, N., *British Shells* (Warne, 1968).

Mellanby, K.M., *Pesticides and Pollution* (Collins, 1967).

Morrell, S.L., 'Sargassum – the lowest form of weed', *Country-Side*, vol. 25, no. 8 (1984).

Murray, I., *Seashore*, Black's Information Books (Black, 1972).

Muss, B.J., and Dahlstrom, P., *Guide to the Sea Fishes of Britain and Northern Europe* (Collins, 1974).

Nelson, B., *Seabirds, their Biology and Ecology* (Hamlyn, 1980).

Ogilvie, M.A., *Ducks of Britain and Europe* (Poyser, 1975).

Ogilvie, M.A., *Wild Geese* (Poyser, 1968).

Patterson, R., *Evolution* (Routledge & Kegan Paul, 1980).

Petersen, R., Mountford, G., and Hallam, P.A.D., *A Field Guide to the Birds of Britain and Europe* (Collins, 1954).

Petpiroon, S., and Dicks, B., 'Environmental effects of effluent discharged into Littlewick Bay, Milford Haven', *Field Studies*, vol. 5, pp. 623–641 (1982).

Prater, A.J., and Davies, M., 'Wintering of sanderlings in Britain', *Bird Study*, vol. 25, pp.33–38 (1978).

Prestt, I., *British Birds: Lifestyles and Habitats* (Batsford, 1982).

Ranwell, D.S., 'Extent of damage to coastal habitats due to the Torrey Canyon incident', in Carthy, J.D., and Arthur, D.R. (eds), *The Biological Effects of Oil Pollution on Littoral Communities*, supplement to *Field Studies*, vol. 2 (1968).

Robinson, A., and Millward, R., *The Shell Book of the British Coast* (David & Charles, 1983).

Savidge, J.P., 'The sand dune flora', in Watkin, E.E., *A Handbook for Ynyslas Nature Reserve* (Nature Conservancy Council, 1976).

South, R., *The Moths of the British Isles* (Warne, vol. 1, 1907, vol. 2, 1908).

Spellerberg, I.F., *Ecological Evaluation for Conservation*, Studies in Biology 133 (Arnold, 1981).

Stamp, Sir Dudley, *Nature Conservation in Britain* (Collins, 1969).

Steers, J.A., *The Coastline of England and Wales* (Collins, 1946).

Swallow, S., *The Seashore Spotter's Guide* (Usbourne, 1978).

Tansley, A.G., *The British Islands and their Vegetation*, vol. 2 (CUP, 1939).

Taylor, J.C., 'The introduction of exotic plant and animal species into Britain', Environmental Review, No. 7, *Biologist*, vol. 26, part 5 (1979).

Tinbergen, N., *The Herring Gull's World* (OUP, 1952).

Tebble, N., *British Bivalve Shells* (HMSO, 1976).

Walker, D., 'Direction and rate in some British post-glacial hydroseres', in Walker, D., and West, R.G. (eds), *The Vegetation of the British Isles* (CUP, 1970).

Wheeler, A., *The Fishes of the British Isles and N.W. Europe* (Macmillan, 1969).

Yonge, C.M., *The Sea Shore* (Collins, 1951).

British Naturalists' Association Guides

Other titles already published in this series (all available from The Crowood Press) are:

Ponds and Streams by John Clegg (1985)

Fields, Farms and Hedgerows by Brian Lee (1985)

Woodlands by John Cloudsley-Thompson (1985)

Mountain and Moorland by Brian Brookes (1985)

Wildlife in Towns by Ron Freethy (1986).

ACKNOWLEDGEMENTS

My thanks to Lesley Richards and Dorothy Clark for typing the manuscript. I am further indebted to Lesley for her critical comments on the work at an early stage; and to Ron Freethy, Peter Leek and Mike Radford for their sensitive and constructive editing of the text.

Thanks are also due to the Bolton Museum for the loan of certain specimens, to Christine Worrell and Derek Bedson for processing some of the black and white illustrations, and to those who have contributed illustrations to this book noted individually below.

The table on page 25 has been reproduced by kind permission of Hodder & Stoughton.

PICTURE CREDITS

Colour and Black & White Photos

Brian Barnes: frontispiece, *pages* 10 (both), 11, 14 (both), 15, 19, 21, 22 (all), 31, 34 (both), 38 (both), 40, 42 (both), 51 (both), 55, 59, 63, 64, 67, 68, 69, 70, 74 (both), 76, 78 (both), 79 (top), 82, 83, 86 (bottom), 92, 95 (both), 96 (right), 98 (both), 99 (top), 102, 103, 106 (both) 110, 114, 115 (top), 117, 118, 119 (top), 122 (both)
Will Bown: *pages* 12, 90 (both)
B. W. Burnett: *page* 18
John Clegg: *pages* 79 (bottom), 100
Michael Edwards: *pages* 81, 87, 96 (left), 99 (bottom), 104, 105 (top), 119 (bottom)
Ron Freethy: *pages* 17, 33, 60, 85 (bottom), 89, 94
E. C. M. Haes: *pages* 16, 105 (bottom)
John Heap: *page* 86 (top)
Alan W. Heath: *pages* 41, 48, 49 (top), 115 (bottom)

Margaret Hodge: *pages* 36, 46, 54
Robert Howe: *page* 26
Charles Linford: *pages* 71, 85 (top), 111
Barry Ogden: *page* 91
D. J. Slynn: *pages* 29, 43, 44, 49 (bottom), 52, 53, 57
Ian Spellerberg: *page* 108
K. Taylor: *page* 121
J. H. Whalley: *pages* 9, 35
Bill Wilkinson: *page* 123

Cover Photos

Top left: Brian Barnes
Top right: Margaret Hodge
Bottom left: Margaret Hodge
Bottom right: Margaret Hodge

Line Drawings

Carole Pugh: *pages* 39, 47, 66, 72, 93

INDEX